The Voice of Things

THE VOICE
OF THINGS

◘ FRANCIS PONGE ◘

EDITED AND TRANSLATED
WITH AN INTRODUCTION
By Beth Archer

McGraw-Hill Book Company

New York ◘ St. Louis ◘ San Francisco

1 2 3 4 5 6 7 8 9 BP BP 7 9 8 7 6 5 4 3 2

FIRST EDITION

Original edition: *Le Parti Pris des Choses*, © 1942 by Éditions Gallimard, Paris; also LE GRAND RECUEIL, vol. I, *Lyres;* vol. II, *Méthodes;* and vol. III, *Pièces*, © 1961 by Éditions Gallimard, Paris; *Nouveau Recueil*, © 1967 by Éditions Gallimard, Paris; *La Fabrique du Pré*, © 1971 by Skira, Geneva.

Library of Congress Cataloging in Publication Data

Ponge, Francis.
    The voice of things.

    Includes the whole of *Le Parti Pris des Choses* and a selection of poems and essays from the author's other works.
    I. Archer, Beth, tr. II. Title.
PQ2631.0643A23   848'.9'1407'   72-3185
ISBN 0-07-073753-3

▣ For V. B. and H. P. ▣

Puisque tu me lis, cher lecteur,
donc je suis; puisque tu nous lis
(mon livre et moi), cher lecteur,
donc nous sommes (Toi, lui et moi).

FRANCIS PONGE

Contents

□ **II. Methods**

□ **III. Pieces**

�«▫» **IV. Lyres**

�«▫» **V. The Prairie**

�«▫» **VI. This Is Why I Have Lived**

The Voice of Things

Introduction

To see the world
   in a grain of sand
And heaven in a wild flower:
Hold infinity in the palm
   of your hand,
And eternity in an hour.
              WILLIAM BLAKE

�«▣» I

Caveat Lector

By way of preface, this is a warning to the reader who
expects prose to be prosaic. To such I would say, *"Stay
away!"* For this is elusive, misleading, perplexing stuff.
The very appearance of Ponge's pages is disorienting.
Written in prose, the orderly lines, grouped familiarly
on the page in everyday paragraphs, suggest immediate
communication. Even the language, at first glance, seems
to be the language of everyday. And what could be more

everyday than the subjects: an orange, a potato, a cigarette, a goat?

A clue to the surreptitious nature of this writing can
be found in the Renaissance view of poetry as something
so wonderful it must be concealed from the common
gaze. Like Holy Scripture, it reveals its mystery to the
wise, but should not be exposed to "the irreverent that
they cheapen [it] not by too common familiarity."[1]
Myths, fables, allegories were therefore used to communicate with the learned reader who knew how to find
the meaning beneath the surface of gods, heroes and
animals. "The poet who associates his hero with Hercules or Achilles shows him . . . in a preexisting heroic
form. At the same time, the poet puts an important part
of his meaning in code [which] will only be understood
by a reader familiar with mythology and with the further
truths it conceals."[2]

In the prose poetry of Francis Ponge, coming as he
does in an un-heroic age fashioned more by scientific
than by classical studies, the direction is down rather
than up, smaller rather than larger. The subjects of his
allegories or fables belong to a lower world than that of
the gods and heroes of antiquity, and are treated zoo-
morphically, as opposed to the anthropomorphism of an
Aesop or a La Fontaine. However, like his Renaissance
antecedents, he too is creating a new humanism. He states
his purpose to be "a description-definition-literary art
work" which, avoiding the drabness of the dictionary
and the inadequacy of poetic description, will lead to a
cosmogony, that is, an account— through the successive

1. Boccaccio, *De Genealogia Deorum,* trans. Charles G. Osgood,
in *Boccaccio on Poetry,* Princeton, Princeton University Press, 1930,
p. 53.
2. Eugene M. Waith, *The Herculean Hero,* New York, Columbia
University Press, 1962, p. 50.

and cumulative stages of linguistic development—of the totality of man's view of the universe and his relationship to it.

Disclaiming any taste or talent for ideas, which disgust him because of their pretension to absolute truth, he abandons ideas and opts for things. In a short piece dating from 1930 entitled "Plus-que-raisons," which would appear to be a phenomenological manifesto, he says:

It is less a matter of truth than the integrity of the mind, and less the integrity of the mind than that of the whole man. No possible compromise between taking the side of ideas or things to be described, and taking the side of words. Given the singular power of words, the absolute power of the established order, only one attitude is possible: taking the side of things all the way.[3]

Ideas then, at least in any conventional philosophic form, are not for him. Since the truth they lay claim to can be invalidated by contradictory ideas, since there is no acquired capital, no solid ground to step on or over, ideas remain in a state of flux, like the sea, and provoke in him a feeling of nausea. This aversion to ideas is discussed at length in a later essay, "My Creative Method,"[4] whose vocabulary (*écoeurement, vague à l'âme, pénible inconsistance, nausée*) irresistibly recalls Sartre's *La Nausée*.

It is of little importance to determine here who influenced whom. The chronology would seem to indicate, if anything, a curious interplay. Some of Ponge's early theorizing dates back to 1922 and 1930 in such essays as "Fragments Métatechniques" and "Plus-que-raisons"; the texts composing *Le Parti Pris des Choses* were written over a period of two decades prior to their publication in 1942; *La Nausée* appeared in 1938; and "My

3. In *Nouveau Recueil*, Paris, Gallimard, 1967, p. 32.
4. Translated in full in this volume.

Creative Method" in 1947. What is interesting is that a line from *La Nausée* such as

> The truth is that I can't/let go of my pen: I think I'm going to be sick [*avoir la nausée*] and have the impression of holding it back by writing. And I write whatever comes to mind.[5]

is echoed, after innumerable repetitions of "ideas provoke in me a kind of nausea," by

> I never said anything except what came into my head at the moment I said it, on the subject of perfectly ordinary things, chosen completely at random.[6]

Sartre's protagonist Roquentin, after laboring for years on an insignificant biography, and experiencing the disgust and despair of humanistic clichés—the empty commonplaces of philosophy, politics, religion, history, that pass themselves off as unalterable truths—rediscovers the little jazz melody "Some of these days," and through it seems to discover the validity of the work of art.

> *It* [the melody; *elle* in French] does not exist. It is beyond, always beyond something, the voice, the note of the violin. Through the many thicknesses of existence, it reveals itself, thin and strong, and when one wants to take hold of it, one only comes upon existents, one stumbles on existents empty of meaning. It does not exist, because there is nothing too much in it: it is everything else that is too much in relation to it. It *is*.[7]

Ponge also discovers the validity of the work of art; and for him too it has an inner life that goes beyond existence:

5. Jean-Paul Sartre, *La Nausée*, Paris, Gallimard, 1938, p. 216.
6. "My Creative Method," in LE GRAND RECUEIL, vol. II, Paris, Gallimard, 1961, p. 38.
7. *La Nausée*, p. 218.

And yet, if one observes carefully, *she* [*The Goat;* also *elle,* and also underlined by the author] lives, *she* moves a bit. If one approaches, she pulls on her rope and tries to flee.

There is nothing to count on, no truth to explain the why's and how's of our existence. But there is the melody, the work of art, and that at least *is.* "So one can justify one's existence?" Roquentin asks, thinking of the poor slob suffering his own anguish on the 20th floor of some New York apartment house as he writes "Some of these days":

Couldn't I try . . . Evidently not a piece of music . . . but in some other way? It would have to be a book: I don't know how to do anything else. But not a history. History talks about what has existed—an existent can never justify the existence of another existent. Another kind of book, I don't know which— one would have to guess, behind the printed words, behind the pages, at something that would not exist but would be above existence.[8]

In "My Creative Method," Ponge writes: "If I must exist . . . it can only be through some creation on my part," and goes on to explain what kind of creation he envisions. For Sartre it is the novel, a multiplicity of words. For Ponge, it is the word, in the singular, which reveals a life beyond its functional existence; a literary creation, yes, but a new form, a poetic encyclopedia that accounts for man's universe, and justifies the creator, through the many thicknesses of the word's existence, "borrowing the brevity and infallibility of the dictionary definition and the sensory aspect of the literary description."

However, it is not to be a hermetic form that exists for its own sake. Ponge is no partisan of art for art. "Of course, the work of art immortally leads its own life,

8. La Nausée, pp. 221–222.

animated by the inner multiplication of references, and the mysterious induction of the soul within the proportions chosen. But wherever there is soul, there is still man."[9] And the artist can proceed by many means to achieve his aim. But the end product, the art work, must be less concerned with mere narration or description of the object, be it a man, an event or a thing, than with the secrets it holds, the multiple notions behind it: "It is less the object that must be painted than an idea of that object."[10] It is 1922 and he still uses the word "idea" ingenuously. Warding off the anticipated accusation of "Romanticism!—it is nature we need instead of ideas, nature and her eternal traits," he replies:

Where do you see them except in yourself, where can I see them except in myself? Nature exists—in us. Beauty exists— in us.[11]

The artist-creator, using nature as God used clay to fashion Adam, fleshes his bare creation with his ideas; clothes it in an artistic form, the chosen genre; uses his style to give expression to the face. This is where language, for the form chosen by Ponge, becomes all important. "One can make fun of Littré, but one has to use his dictionary. Besides current usage, he provides the most convenient source of etymology. What science is more necessary to the poet?"[12] Words are the raw material of poetry, containing in themselves a beauty which the poet can release, just as particular blocks of marble are both material and inspiration for the sculptor, the cut or grain of the piece suggesting its ultimate form.

9. "Fragments Métatechniques," in *Nouveau Recueil*, p. 16.
10. *Ibid.*, p. 17.
11. *Ibid.*, p. 17.
12. *Ibid.*, p. 15.

In *Le Parti Pris des Choses*,[13] which is the entrance
gate to Ponge's domain, one sees these blocks of marble
in miniature. The orange, the oyster, the snail, the
pebble, are not merely described; they emerge as do
figures from stone, characters from the novel. "It is less
a matter of observing the pebble than installing oneself
in its heart and seeing the world with its eyes, like the
novelist who, in order to portray his heroes, lets himself
sink into their consciousness and describes things and
people as they appear to them. This position allows one
to understand why Ponge calls his work a cosmogony
rather than a cosmology. Because it is not a matter of
describing."[14]

"The Oyster" (p. 37 of this volume) provides a fair
sample of the Ponge method, which, alas, no translation
can render fully. For Ponge is really using the *French*
language, with all its particular characteristics—visual,
vernacular, grammatical, etymological, phonetic, etc.
The raw material here is the noun *huître*, whose circumflex followed by the letters *t, r, e* determine the choice
of descriptive adjectives: *blanchâtre* (whitish), *opiniâtre*
(stubborn), *verdâtre* (greenish), *noirâtre* (blackish).
Now endowed with size, color, character and even vulnerability ("it is a world stubbornly closed, but it can
be opened")—its intrinsic characteristics—Ponge goes
on to its broader aspects, its external significance. Its
"stubbornly closed world" is expanded into "a whole
world to eat and drink." In its literal twofold meaning,
it is both the specific liquid-solid delicacy immediately
available to the palate, and the representative of the

13. Translated here in full under the title of *Taking the Side of
Things*.
14. Jean-Paul Sartre, "L'Homme et les choses," in *Situations I*,
Paris, Gallimard, 1947.

liquid-solid universe which in a larger time-scheme provides us with nourishment. In its figurative meaning, also twofold, it becomes the perfect subject-object. And the duality of the subject-object, the description-art work, is expressed by the twin shell, the "skies above and the skies below," the "*firmament*" (a reference to an ancient notion of a solid covering over the earth) and "the puddle," shimmering "nacre" and "a viscous greenish blob." It is both a thing of beauty in itself—the animal, its objective description, and an artistic creation—the pearl, the thing created by the oyster; the poem, the thing created by the poet. Yet some may see it merely as a blotch on the page, edged with the "blackish lace" of printed letters. In a final remove, the poet views his creation as also having a life of its own "that ebbs and flows on sight" —objective observation of the reader, "and smell"— subjective response to the poem; then views himself as showing off his stylistic gifts at the expense of the authentic thing, snatching the pearl to adorn himself. The small form, the globule produced by the oyster (in French the pun is more evident: *formule* is a small form as well as a formula), has become the little work formed by the poet.

The very title of the collection, *Le Parti Pris des Choses,* contains all the linguistic, semantic and ideological ambiguities of Ponge's entire oeuvre, and deserves some of the same exegesis as the texts. "Taking the side of things," though the commonly accepted translation, is inadequate because it neglects the basic ambiguity of the title: *parti pris des choses* can be the "parti pris" *for* things, but it can also be the "parti pris" *of* things. *Parti pris,* in its primary meaning, is an inflexible decision, a consequence of will and intellect. In common usage, it has come to mean an arbitrary choice of one thing over another, a partiality, a bias. Ponge uses the expression in both aspects of its primary meaning: 1) the poet's option for things over ideas, and 2) the will expressed by the things themselves. The first is elucidated at considerable length in his methodological writings (two of which, "My Creative Method" and "The Silent World Is Our Only Homeland," appear here; others, such as *La Rage de l'Expression, Pour un Malherbe, Le Savon,* which are whole volumes, combine method and poetic practice).

The second primary meaning has to be gleaned from the more strictly poetical writings. Snails, trees, flowers, pebbles, the sea, all express an indomitable will, a striving for self-perfection, a single-minded purpose, that assumes heroic proportions combining the excesses and self-mastery characteristic of the noblest of mythological heroes. The wrathful fury of a Hercules or an Ajax is echoed by the tree's rage for expression as it floods the world with more and more leaves, the snail's proud drivel that remains stamped on everything, the rose's excessive petals, the shrimp's persistent return to the same places. Yet in their weakness, their extravagant expressions of self, lie the makings of their greatness, as Hercules' domination of his anger and other heroes' control of their mortal fear lead to god-like valor. Conquering the apparent futility of their acts, their vulnerability, their mortality, by continuing their efforts, they brave destiny by becoming more of what they are. "They are heroes," Ponge says in "The Snail," "beings whose existence is itself a work of art."

Beyond the connotation of option and will lies a more concealed and more complex implication in the arbitrary, partial quality of the expression as it is commonly used. Man, arbitrarily placed in the world, makes an arbitrary choice allowing him to survive in it, before being arbitrarily removed from it, like the crate, used only once and then tossed on the trash heap. The poet, having chosen literature to make his life meaningful, uses words which can only partially convey his meaning, as his art, or the work of any man, can only partially express the man—or man the cosmos.

◘ II

Where "The Oyster" offered us a succinct example of Ponge's art, the universe in a shell so to speak, "The Goat" provides us with a vast panorama of man in the universe and of Ponge's artistry. Here we see the magnifying process of Ponge's lens.

The poem begins with a seemingly unpretentious description of the goat, a pathetic beast dragging a swollen udder, a patch of dark hair across her rump, grazing on the sparse though aromatic grasses that grow between the barren rocks, her little bell clanging as she moves.

In that short opening, Ponge has stated all his themes. The goat is at once revealed as a metaphor for the poet, and in a broader sense for man—and everything she is, wears and does relates to a totality of man's view of himself. In the first line we are still looking *at* the goat, commiserating with *her* plight. But in the fourth line, a single word, *"la pauvresse"* (the poor thing), determines our real optic. We, looking *through* the goat, are moved because we see ourselves as the poet in a harsh world, carrying around the milk of human thought—reason, artistic creation—nurtured by the meager aliment of words, those "nibblings." Insignificant? That is what most people would say. But these tenacious trifles—words, thoughts, poems—are what last after all. The goat, as a work of art, lives on; *"she* lives, *she* moves."

And she really does move. Beginning with the never ceasing bell, she leads us rapidly into the world behind us. The bell, like a call to prayer, and the goat's belief in the grace surrounding her offspring, evoke Mary and her divine infant, and even more broadly, man's belief that he is made in the image of God. Like the kid, he is always reaching higher than his condition, and capricious (a pun that works in English; from *capra,* goat), headstrong, ready to affront anything with his minuscule means—the kid, his horns; man, his mind.

"Untiring wet-nurses, remote princesses, like the galaxies" leads us even farther back, to Greek mythology. Hera, eternal milk-giver, was duped by Zeus into nursing Hercules to make him immortal. When she suddenly withdrew in pain, her milk splattered across the sky and became the Milky Way.[15] This allusion, sandwiched between Christian references, is not the artistic *non sequitur* it would seem to be. For Hercules and Jesus became fused in Renaissance thinking, and for reasons apparent to anyone familiar with the Herculean myth.

Zeus begat Hercules to have a son powerful enough to protect the gods and men from destruction. Alcmene, a mortal like Mary, was carefully selected for her genealogy as well as her virtues to bear him. Hercules, though immortalized by Hera's milk, had to achieve his godhood through his labors which freed the world of monsters and tyrants. The notion of the world's redemption through the divine hero's suffering (The Labors, The Passion) and self-mastery (Hercules' anger, Jesus'

15. Another detail in the myth that curiously relates to the poem is Hera's epithet of "goat-eating," coming perhaps from Hercules' sacrifice of goats when raising a temple to her at Sparta. (Robert Graves, *The Greek Myths*, Baltimore, Penguin Books, 1955, vol. II, p. 186).

temptation in the desert) provides a striking link between these two god-begotten figures. And linked to them is man, who through his gift of intellect and his mortal anguish also seeks some manner of redemption. Hercules' victories were seen in the Renaissance as the triumph of the mind over vice, and his slaying of the Nemean lion was interpreted as the domination of anger. The lion skin, which he continued to wear as invulnerable armor, came to symbolize reason, man's unique armor. "Perfect yourself morally, and you will produce beautiful verses. First know yourself. In keeping with your lines."—is the lesson Ponge seriocomically draws from the snail. The goat's rug that passes for a shawl evokes the lion skin, but on the downtrodden goat-man, it is a pathetic tatter, a remnant of past glory, perhaps a reminder to continue striving.

Although Ponge preaches phenomenology and accepts the label of "materialist"—which some of his admirers use to distinguish his work from the politically tainted literature of bourgeois humanism—he himself recognizes his debt to Rimbaud and Mallarmé who come out of an idealist tradition. And since the "thingliness" he practices does not function in a vacuum, he further recognizes that "everything written moralizes." It is in this connection that the allegorical nature of his poems appears. In so far as these works utilize animals and things to point to a veiled meaning, they are fables. But they are not conventional fables, in that their *purpose* is not to moralize. They neither condemn immorality nor advocate virtue—except perhaps in the sense of existentialist virtue, or the *virtus* of antiquity, both of which are self-achieved and self-discovered. They are perhaps more in the nature of a modern fairy tale, like Orwell's *Animal Farm*, which moves the reader precisely through its dispassionate tone, its absence of direct appeal. On the level of the fairy tale, Ponge is offering us a view of life transcribed into mute symbols, whose function is to "express (the object's) mute character, its lesson, in almost moral terms." However, unlike Orwell, he is not portraying man's incorrigible nature. Quite the contrary. He is showing us that the condition of life is mortality, but in death there is life: from the corpse of one culture another is born, carrying with it, through words, the chromosomes and genes of the past. The pebble, final offspring of a race of giants, is of the same stone as its enormous forebears. And if life offers no faith, no truth, it nonetheless offers possibilities. For trees there may be no way out of their treehood "by the means of trees"—leaves wither and fall—but they do not give up, they go on leafing season after season. They are not resigned. This is the first "lesson," the heroic vision, and the first weapon against mortality. The second is the creative urge, the "will to formation" and the perfection of whatever means are unique to the individual: the tree has leaves, the snail its silver wake, man his words. He also possesses all the "virtues" of the world he lives in: the fearful fearlessness of the shrimp, the stubbornness of the oyster, the determination of water, the cigarette's ability to create its own environment and its own destruction. The ultimate weapon is the work of art, the sublime regenerative possibility, which man carries within himself like the oyster its pearl, the orange its pip. These are not "morals" in any strict didactic sense, but they are lessons, of the kind that the Renaissance learned from antiquity—models of exemplary virtue to follow.

Returning to "The Goat," the poem continues its Christian metaphor with the key words that follow. "Kneeling," "decrucifying their stiff limbs"—the goat now plural, hence all men—"starry-eyed" with a memory of paradise and the hope of redemption, "they do

not forget their duty" for there is no repose any longer.
They have tasted of Beelzebub ("hairy as beasts," "Beelzebumptious") and know the torment of mortality, now
bound to their human condition like the goat to its
tether, "rope at the end of its rope, a rope whip"—the
Flagellation—cast out "to haunt rocky places."

The milk, once of immortality, now of knowledge,
tastes of "flint," the brimstone of hell, Satan's touch. Yet
it is still life-giving in its dual generative qualities of
milk-milt, intellect and semen; "readily convulsive in
his deep sacks"—the milky lobes of the brain, the semen-
laden glands, also dual. Burdened with consciousness
and desire, man is both Goat-Satyr and Goat-Satan. Like
Satan, man was cast out and seeks to regain his lofty
place by reaching ever higher, *ad astra per aspera,* but
like the goat, powerless, sacrificial victim, he cannot go
beyond the topmost crags of his futile climb to immortality—"no triumphal soaring." "Brought closer and
closer by [his] researches," he discovers it leads nowhere he can go, and he has "to back down to the first
bush"—like Sisyphus, to begin all over again. This is
yet another reason why we are so moved by the sight of the
goat, this "miserable accident, sordid adaptation to sordid
contingencies, and in the end nothing but shreds"—
the history of human achievement, from Pericles to
potsherds, Deuteronomy to Dachau.

So that we can hardly take pride in this milk of our
reason, or the progeny of our seed, though it is for us to
use—and all we have—as a means of "some obscure regeneration, by way of the kid and the goat": our successive creations.

"The Goat" is a prime example of Ponge's semantic
genius. Every word is a signpost pointing in all direc-
tions, and every word construction a vast game—like
children's board games that lead one around a circuit

of pitfalls and repeated beginnings to some marvelous finish line—an endlessly fascinating game, like the game of life itself, with the reward just beyond reach. The tools of his game are the dictionary, an inexhaustible memory for historical, literary and pictorial references, archaisms, neologisms, even barbarisms when necessary—and countless puns, which make translating Ponge something of a sport: hunting, to be precise. Since Latin is a parent common to both languages, it is sometimes possible to come away with a genuine trophy. At other times, one has to make do with an approximation—antlers bought from a taxidermist.

Not an occasion is lost. He starts from the very first sentence: ". . . because between her frail legs she carries . . ." The French reads: *pource qu'elle comporte,* *pource* being the fusing of *bourse* (bag, sack) with *pour ce que* (for the reason that); *comporte* means "carries with" but it also means "connotes." There are innumerable puns on the "goatliness" of the subject: variations on *cornes,* horns—*cornemuse,* bagpipe; *corniaud,* "knucklehead" coming closest to the idea of an antlered fool; *têtu,* headstrong; *il fait front,* he affronts anything, from *front,* forehead, *faire front,* face squarely up to something; *entre deux coups de boutoir,* between two sallies, from *bouter,* to push or drive out, and *buter,* come up against (an obstacle), *boutoir,* a sharp retort, a witticism ("sally" in English carries a similar double meaning of a sudden forward thrust and a witty remark), and finally *buté,* the adjective derived from *buter,* obstinate—all of which summons the image of relentless butting.

The short passage in which both sound and meaning are joined in a brilliant goatly cadenza deserves to be quoted in the original (translation on p. 136 of this volume):

> Ces belles aux longs yeux, poilues commes des bêtes,
> belles à la fois et butées—ou, pour mieux dire,
> belzébuthées—quand elles bêlent, de quoi se plaignent-
> elles? de quel tourment, quel tracas?

Not only are all the characteristics of the goat as animal and symbol utilized; Ponge even finds inspiration in the spelling of the noun, *chèvre*. Its grave accent marks the goat's seriousness and low-pitched bleat, and serves as a humorous criticism of his own "psalmodizing." And its last syllable, that suspended consonant with its mute "e" hanging in mid-air, furnishes him with an invented pun, *la muette*, from the feminine for *muet*, mute, and *la mouette*, the gull or mew. The goat has been examined in all its aspects: goat-hero, goat-Satan, goat-satyr, tragic goat-man, and even comic goat-man, the paper- and tobacco-loving old bachelor.

Despite its shortcomings, its shabbiness—another pun: *loque fautive*, faulty tatter; *fautif* suggests both defectiveness and guilt—its pitifulness and uselessness, it is still a marvelous thing because it functions, it produces, it *is*. Man, this "magnificent knucklehead," weighed down by his grandiose ideas, knows that deep within him are love and reason. He is free to become—beast or hero, derelict or artist. Reason remains, so does the work of art, and with it perhaps "some obscure regeneration."

▣ III

Since it is impossible to analyze all of Ponge's works, and meaningless to indulge in generalities without textual examples, I have selected "The Oyster," "The

Goat" and "The Prairie" as significant samples of Ponge's art. There are, of course, others and in particular two which do not appear in this volume, "L'Araignée" ("The Spider"), already admirably translated by Mark Temmer,[16] and "Le Soleil Placé en Abîme," which runs to thirty-eight pages and is consequently too long to be included here.

"The Prairie" ("Le Pré"), in that it incorporates all of Ponge's ideas, techniques, sensibility and eccentricity, seems to me his magnum opus to date. First published in 1967 in *Nouveau Recueil* (the last volume of his collected works to appear in the Gallimard edition), it has recently been reprinted in a handsome Skira edition, along with the journal Ponge kept during the four years of its composition and which provides the title, "La Fabrique du Pré" ("The Making of the Prairie"). It is a fascinating, albeit tedious, account of the poem's genesis and the poet's thought process.

Ponge's approbation, and appropriation, of nature; his awareness of himself as spectator and participant in an exterior world; his equally keen awareness of the reality of the verbal world of language, as valid and as external as the physical world, all reach their apogee in this poem. We see here concretized and poeticized the dual genealogies that run parallel throughout Ponge's work: the course of human, vegetable or mineral evolution, and its counterpart in the semantic history of words, the evolution of meaning.

The ultimate achievement for Ponge would be for each word composing a text to be taken in each of its successive connotations throughout history. This, were it possible, would be not just the tracing of language in a historical, philological sense, but the consecration of a

16. In *Prairie Schooner*, 1966.

birth to death rite which goes beyond the word to creation itself.

The creative urge, like the reproductive urge, is a
movement toward death, in the sense of the self ex-
pended, and with the same goal: the birth of a new
entity. The need to bridge the silence of mortality is the
desire to fulfill one's function.

The relationship between Eros and Thanatos is evident, and
death in this sense is part of life. I have often insisted on the
fact that it is necessary in some way to die in order to give
birth to something, or someone, and I am not the first to have
seen that the birth of a text can only occur through the death
of the author. The sex act, the act of reproduction, also requires
the presence of another. The two must die, more or less, for the
third person, in this case the text, to be born. The second
person for me is the thing, the object that provoked the desire
and that also dies in the process of giving birth to the text.
There is thus, at the same time, the death of the author and
the death of the object of the desire—the thing, the pre-text.[17]

In "Le Pré" the process is vividly metaphorized. "J'ai
d'abord eu, une fois . . . une émotion me venant d'un
pré, au sens de prairie," Ponge explains. Beginning then
with the emotion produced by the physical object, the
prairie, he seeks to fix it, eternalize it, by writing it, for
fear of losing it. His concern, at first, is merely to express it, render it, as would a landscape painter, using
words in place of paint. The word *pré* itself, however,
soon becomes obsessive. It recurs everywhere, in every
form; a simple phoneme whose implications far exceed
its nominative function. Consulting the dictionary, Ponge
discovers that "in fact, it is one of the most important
roots existing in French."[18] "Why?" he goes on, "because *pré, le pré, la prairie,* come from the Latin

17. *Entretiens de Francis Ponge avec Philippe Sollers,* Paris,
Gallimard/Seuil, 1970, p. 171.
18. *Ibid.,* pp. 172–173.

pratum, which Latin etymologists consider a crasis, a contraction of *paratum—that which has been prepared*."

Pré, then, as what has been made ready, has occurred before, implies a past-ness that gives the noun *pré-prairie* the significance of something previously prepared by nature—for food, for rest, for life—in all its organic spectrum; a perpetual rebirth of plant, animal and man; a continuity of the life cycle; man lives on animals that live on grass that lives on their remains. However, *paratum-pré*, the anterior preparation, or what Ponge calls "le participe passé par excellence," does not remain fixed in the past since it becomes *pré-prairie*, which exists in the present. Even the prefix,[19] implying what comes before, also indicates something to follow: precede, predict, preface, all point to some future quality or event. The simple phoneme, whether noun or prefix, consequently embodies the whole spectrum of time as well—past, present, future.

The *pré*, be it field, meadow or prairie, is both the prelude to life as a place of nourishment, and a presage of death as a place of encounter. *Pré-aux-clercs*, the clerics' or scholars' field, meeting-place for medieval preceptors and students, the place of discussion and disputation, became the place of decision, the field of action, the dueling ground. Two vertical figures meet on a grassy field, cross swords in oblique thrusts, until one

19. *Pre*, an equally important prefix in English, and *prairie*, which exists identically in both languages, and which Ponge uses repeatedly as a synonym for the noun *pré*), allow for a translation that does not alter the multiple meanings of the original. *Meadow* might be more precise a translation of *pré* but its Middle English derivation and completely unrelated sound would render the very germ of the poem unintelligible. The prefix, though also resulting from a crasis, derives in fact from *prae*, but that does not invalidate Ponge's homonymic use of it. What Ponge means by "participe passé" is the spelling of the word *pré*, whose accented "e" is the ending of the past participle in first conjugation verbs.

or both fall horizontally on the ground, first lying on top of the grassy surface, then buried beneath it. This scene, appearing in four lines in the poem, is also symbolic of the creative process, the duel between the author and the object of the creative urge, both ending in the creation, *Le Pré*, which remains in an eternal present.

A certain graphic quality, arising perhaps from Ponge's initial impetus to render the prairie as landscape, is maintained throughout the poem, all the while moving out of nature into the works of man. Green is spread on a page, a small quadrangle, the words surging up from a brown page as grass rises out of the earth; a horizontal fragment of limited space, barely larger than a handkerchief, pelted by vertical storms and adverse signs, as the page, about the size of a handkerchief, is struck by vertical, horizontal and oblique signs of type. The earth regains the surface through the trampled grass, as the physical object, prairie, reappears through words: man's greening, regenerative faculty. The long procession of strollers in their Sunday finery recalls Seurat's *Grande Jatte*, where on the stippled green of the canvas banks they cannot soil their shoes.

The mysterious interjection, "Why then from the start does it prohibit us?" and the lines that follow (p. 180 of this volume), seem also to refer to painting. Seurat's *Grande Jatte* and Manet's *Déjeuner sur l'herbe* can reproduce through color, light and form, the mood and the scene of those green expanses. But the poet, having only words, is held back, inhibited by his scruples, prohibited from the celebration. (In French, the interjection quoted above reads "pourquoi nous tient-il interdits": *interdire* implies bewilderment, but also restriction in the Catholic sense of a prohibition against performing certain rites—"Could we then already be at the naos," that part of the Greek temple where only priests were permitted.) "That sacred place for a repast of reasons" ("lieu sacré d'un petit déjeuné de raisons")[20] evokes Manet's *Déjeuner sur l'herbe,* in which the food scattered among the folds of the crumpled cloth suggests that the repast is over, and the nude young woman, contrasting with the reasoning gesture of one of her male companions, suggests the discussion will also soon be over. "Here we are then, at the heart of pleonasms" —verbal redundancies, the poet's only logical possibility. The sanctity of the place is guaranteed by nature and the poet; no need for "prosternating" to any higher power, for such a horizontal movement would conflict with the "verticalities of the place," the upright sufficiency of grass, trees, hedges, and the words of the poem.

And "did the original storm," the creative urge which rivals the divine, "not thunder" within the poet so that he would leave behind all fear and formality, and produce a truth commensurate with the objective reality, a "verdant verity" in which he could revel, having fulfilled his nature? "The bird flying over it in the opposite direction to writing" reminds him of the concrete reality which his poem only approximates, and of the contradiction inherent in the word *pré* with its multiple levels of meaning and time. And from the pleasurable image of a blue sky seen overhead while reclining on the grassy surface, he turns to the final rest beneath the same surface. Coming to an abrupt end, as does life itself, he places himself beneath the poem,

20. Ponge's use of the rarer "déjeuné" for "déjeuner" seems to indicate an intent to give adjective and noun their full value of "little lunch" or light repast, rather than the locution "petit déjeuner" meaning breakfast. "Déjeuner sur l'herbe" would be translated today as "picnic."

through which his name will flower like the herbs above his grave.

◻ IV

There would seem to be no way out of ambiguity. Man cannot escape the ambiguity of his immortal spirit in a mortal condition, nor the poet the ambiguities of language by means of words, and the critic is enmeshed in them when talking about a writer like Ponge. Even his chosen métier is ambiguous. He steadfastly refuses to consider himself a poet, or his writing poetry; at most he grants it the name of "prôemes." Yet these short pieces, even the ones on art, are undeniably poetic. He admits he "uses poetic magma" but hastily adds, "only to get rid of it." Just as he insists that "ideas are not my forte," yet ideas spring out of each page in dizzying profusion. And everything points to man—his formidable capacity for renewal, the glory of his mind and soul, albeit in a non-religious yet strongly metaphysical context. "The veneration of matter: what can be worthier of the spirit? Whereas the spirit venerating spirit . . ."

And so, he is a would-be encyclopedist compiling poetic language; a would-be materialist composing metaphysical texts in the least concrete of media; an anti-idealist who, like the plant that only uses the world as a mine for its protoplasm, digs into humanist culture merely for raw material, but evolves a neo-humanism combining classical techniques with romantic self-awareness; a fabulist who ridicules his moralizing; a Renaissance craftsman who uses modern science to fashion jewels—and all part of a search for beauty that probably exasperates his new-found supporters among the cultural Maoists.

What Ponge is offering us is a taste of genuine culture, a synthesis of past and present, and at a time when sub- and counter-cultures are dulling our senses. Just as strings have been humiliated into making percussive sounds, and rhythms have been reduced to a hallucinating throb, so words have been simplified to the level of Orff instruments, limited to elementary meanings as are they to elementary sounds. In place of uniform bricks for factories, Ponge has unearthed varied material for palaces and temples, be they no larger than a snail shell.

And finally, he constructs a cosmogony which turns out to be an account not of the origin, but of the agony of the cosmos—an agony of joy as well as an agony of death. One has a feeling of eternal resurgence and surprise, each word like Chinese boxes opening one into the other, each text a fresh attempt to seize a fragment of the universe. If there is any graphic symbol to characterize Ponge, it would be the circle—the cycle of the seasons, the sea-rounded pebble, the orange, the plate—but above all, the circularity of his technique. He begins with the word, which inspires the form, which constructs the idea, which determines the word. In the beginning was the word, and in the end as well.

B. A.

Honfleur, New Haven, 1971

Translator's Note

This collection is necessarily limited to a mere sampling of the more than two thousand pages of Ponge's published writings. It is intended to serve as an introduction to his work, and as such cannot be all things to all people. The choices, arbitrary of course, were made with an eye to the reader whose French is not fluent, and to some manner of unity. Ponge's esthetic side seemed more important than the many others to be found in his vast production. Works that depend too heavily on linguistic devices, are too rooted in a French critical context, or are already well translated, were eliminated in favor of shorter, more translatable, less hermetic pieces. There are many beautiful pieces, such as *Le Verre d'eau,* which had to be left out for these reasons, as there are beautiful lines, such as "parfois par temps à peine un peu plus fort clamée" from *Seashores,* that could not be rendered in comparable sound and rhythm. I have tried to avoid the traditional charge of *traduttore-traditore* by remaining as faithful as possible to the spirit, if not always the letter of the text. The Latinate terms Ponge is fond of, which could be taken for a heaviness of translation, were simplified: words such as "caduque" and "superfétatoire," though existing in both languages, were replaced by "fast-falling" and "twice-spawned." The humor of such pedantry, to which any alumnus of the French lycée would be sensitive, runs the risk of falling flat in English.

To Francis Ponge, my thanks for this intimate relationship with his work; to Henri Peyre, my thanks for having made it possible; and to my husband, Victor Brombert, my thanks for his short-tempered replies which made me look farther and work harder, and for his rare praise which I could trust.

1

Taking the Side of Things

(Complete*)

* *Le Parti Pris des Choses,* Paris, Gallimard, 1942. "La Crevette" ("The Shrimp") originally appeared in *Le Parti Pris des Choses.* It was later reprinted in *La Crevette dans Tous Ses États,* and to avoid repetition, appears only on p. 128 of the present volume, as "Shrimp Two." (All notes, unless otherwise indicated, are the translator's.)

▣ Rain

Rain, in the courtyard where I watch it fall, comes down at very different speeds. At the center it is a sheer uneven curtain (or net), an implacable but relatively slow descent of fairly light drops, an endless precipitation without vigor, a concentrated fraction of the total meteor. Not far from the walls to the right and left, heavier individuated drops fall more noisily. Here they seem the size of wheat kernels, there large as peas, elsewhere big as marbles. Along the window sills and mouldings the rain streaks horizontally, while on the underside of these obstacles it hangs suspended like lozenges. It ripples along, thinly coating the entire surface of a little zinc roof beneath my glance, moiréed with the various currents caused by the imperceptible rises and falls of the covering. From the nearby gutter, where it flows with the effort of a shallow brook poorly sloped, it plummets sharply to the ground in a perfectly vertical, thickly corded trickle where it shatters and rebounds like glistening icicles.

Each of its forms has a particular speed, accompanied by a particular sound. All of it runs with the intensity of a complex mechanism, as precise as it is unpredictable, like a clockwork whose mainspring is the weight of a given mass of precipitating vapor.

The pealing of the vertical jets on the ground, the gurgling of the gutters, the tiny gong strokes, multiply and resound together in a concert neither monotonous nor unsubtle.

When the mainspring has unwound, some wheels go on turning for a while, more and more slowly, until the whole machinery stops. Should the sun then reappear, everything is soon effaced; the glimmering mechanism evaporates: it has rained.

▣ The End of Autumn

In the end, autumn is no more than a cold infusion. Dead leaves of all essences steep in the rain. No fermentation, no resulting alcohol: the effect of compresses applied to a wooden leg will not be felt till spring.

The stripping is messily done. All the doors of the reading room fly open and shut, slamming violently. Into the basket, into the basket! Nature tears up her manuscripts, demolishes her library, furiously thrashes her last fruits.

She suddenly gets up from her work table; her height at once immense. Unkempt, she keeps her head in the mist. Arms dangling, she rapturously inhales the icy wind that airs her thoughts. The days are short, night falls fast, there is no time for comedy.

The earth, amid the other planets in space, regains its seriousness. Its lighted side is narrower, infiltrated by valleys of shadow. Its shoes, like a tramp's, slosh and squeak.

In this frog pond, this salubrious amphibiguity, everything regains strength, hops from rock to rock, and moves on to another meadow. Rivulets multiply.

That is what is called a thorough cleaning, and with no respect for conventions! Garbed in nakedness, drenched to the marrow.

And it lasts, does not dry immediately. Three months of healthy reflection in this condition; no vascular reaction, no bathrobe, no scrubbing brush. But its hearty constitution can take it.

And so, when the little buds begin to sprout again, they know what they are up to and what is going on—

and if they peek out cautiously, all numb and flushed, they know why.

But here begins another tale, thereby hanging perhaps but not smelling like the black rule that will serve to draw my line under this one.

▣ Poor Fishermen

Short of haulers, two chains constantly drawing the impasse toward them on the canal, the kids standing around near the baskets were shouting:

"Poor fishermen!"

Here is the summary made to the lampposts:

"Half the fish lost flopping into the sand, three quarters of the crabs back out to sea."

▣ Rum of the Ferns

From beneath the ferns and their lovely little girls do I get a perspective of Brazil?

Neither lumber for building, nor sticks for matches: odd leaves piled on the ground moistened by aged rum.

Sprouting, pulsating stems, prodigal virgins without guardians: an enormous binge of palms completely out of control, each one hiding two-thirds of the sky.

◎   **Blackberries**

On the typographical bushes constituted by the poem,
along a road leading neither away from things nor to the
spirit, certain fruits are formed of an agglomeration of
spheres filled by a drop of ink.

*   *   *

Black, pink, khaki all together on the cluster, they
offer the spectacle of a haughty family of varying ages
rather than a keen temptation to pick them.

Given the disproportion between seeds and pulp, birds
care little for them, since in the end so little is left once
through from beak to anus.

*   *   *

But the poet during his professional stroll is left with
something: "This," he says to himself, "is the way a
fragile flower's patient efforts succeed for the most part,
very fragile though protected by a forbidding tangle of
thorns. With few other qualities—blackberries, black
as ink—just as this poem was made."

◎   **The Crate**

Halfway between *cage* (cage) and *cachot* (cell) the
French language has *cageot* (crate), a simple openwork
case for the transport of those fruits that invariably fall
sick over the slightest suffocation.

Put together in such a way that at the end of its use it

can be easily wrecked, it does not serve twice. Thus it is even less lasting than the melting or murky produce it encloses.

On all street corners leading to the market, it shines with the modest gleam of whitewood. Still brand new, and somewhat taken aback at being tossed on the trash pile in an awkward pose with no hope of return, this is a most likable object all considered—on whose fate it is perhaps wiser not to dwell too long.

◨ The Candle

On occasion night revives an unusual plant whose glow rearranges furnished rooms into masses of shadow.

Its leaf of gold stands impassive in the hollow of a little alabaster column on a very black pedicel.

Mothy butterflies assault it in place of the too high moon that mists the woods. But burned at once, or worn out by the struggle, they all tremble on the brink of a frenzy close to stupor.

Meanwhile, the candle, by the flickering of its rays on the book in the sudden release of its own smoke, encourages the reader—then leans over on its stand and drowns in its own aliment.

◨ The Cigarette

First let us present the atmosphere—hazy, dry, disordered—in which the cigarette is always placed sideways from the time it began creating it.

Then its person: a tiny torch far less luminous than odorous, from which a calculable number of small ash masses splinter and fall, according to a rhythm to be determined.

Finally its martyrdom: a glowing tip, scaling off in silver flakes, the newest ones forming a close muff around it.

▣   The Orange

Like the sponge, the orange aspires to regain face after enduring the ordeal of expression. But where the sponge always succeeds, the orange never does; for its cells have burst, its tissues are torn. While the rind alone is flabbily recovering its form, thanks to its resilience, an amber liquid has oozed out, accompanied, as we know, by sweet refreshment, sweet perfume—but also by the bitter awareness of a premature expulsion of pips as well.

Must one take sides between these two poor ways of enduring oppression? The sponge is only a muscle and fills up with air, clean or dirty water, whatever: a vile exercise. The orange has better taste, but is too passive —and this fragrant sacrifice . . . is really too great a kindness to the oppressor.

However, merely recalling its singular manner of perfuming the air and delighting its tormentor is not saying enough about the orange. One has to stress the glorious color of the resulting liquid which, more than lemon juice, makes the larynx open widely both to pronounce the word and ingest the juice without any apprehensive grimace of the mouth or raising of papillae.

And one remains speechless to declare the well-deserved admiration of the covering of the tender, fragile, russet oval ball inside that thick moist blotter, whose extremely thin but highly pigmented skin, bitterly flavorful, is just uneven enough to catch the light worthily on its perfect fruit form.

At the end of too brief a study, conducted as roundly as possible, one has to get down to the pip. This seed, shaped like a miniature lemon, is the color of the lemon tree's whitewood outside, and inside is the green of a pea or tender sprout. It is within this seed that one finds —after the sensational explosion of the Chinese lantern of flavors, colors and perfumes which is the fruited ball itself—the relative hardness and greenness (not entirely tasteless, by the way) of the wood, the branch, the leaf; in short, the puny albeit prime purpose of the fruit.

◻ The Oyster

The oyster, about as big as a fair-sized pebble, is rougher, less evenly colored, brightly whitish. It is a world stubbornly closed. Yet it can be opened: one must hold it in a cloth, use a dull jagged knife, and try more than once. Avid fingers get cut, nails get chipped: a rough job. The repeated pryings mark its cover with white rings, like haloes.

Inside one finds a whole world, to eat and drink;

under a *firmament* (properly speaking) of nacre, the skies above collapse on the skies below, forming nothing but a puddle, a viscous greenish blob that ebbs and flows on sight and smell, fringed with blackish lace along the edge.

Once in a rare while a globule pearls in its nacre throat, with which one instantly seeks to adorn oneself.

◻ The Pleasures of the Door

Kings do not touch doors.

They know nothing of this pleasure: pushing before one gently or brusquely one of those large familiar panels, then turning back to replace it—holding a door in one's arms.

. . The pleasure of grabbing the midriff of one of these tall obstacles to a room by its porcelain node; that short clinch during which movement stops, the eye widens, and the whole body adjusts to its new surrounding.

With a friendly hand one still holds on to it, before closing it decisively and shutting oneself in—which the click of the tight but well-oiled spring pleasantly confirms.

◻ Trees Undo Themselves Within a Sphere of Fog

In the fog around the trees, they are divested of their leaves which, abashed by slow oxidation and mortified by the sap's abandon in favor of fruits and flowers, had already become less attached ever since the searing heat of August.

Vertical trenches furrow the bark through which moisture is led all the way to the ground to disinterest itself from the vital parts of the trunk.

The flowers have been scattered, the fruits torn down. From earliest youth, giving up their vital qualities and bodily parts has become a familiar practice for trees.

▣ Bread

The surface of a crusty bread is marvelous, first because of the almost panoramic impression it makes: as though one had the Alps, the Taurus or the Andes at one's fingertips.

It so happened that an amorphous mass about to explode was slid into the celestial oven for us where it hardened and formed valleys, summits, rolling hills, crevasses . . . And from then on, all those planes so neatly joined, those fine slabs where light carefully beds down its rays—without a thought for the unspeakable mush underneath.

That cold flaccid substratum is made up of sponge-like tissue: leaves or flowers like Siamese twins soldered together elbow to elbow. When bread grows stale, these flowers fade and wither; they fall away from each other and the mass becomes crumbly . . .

But now let's break it up: for in our mouths bread should be less an object of respect than one of consumption.

▣ Fire

Fire has a system: first all the flames move in one direction . . .

(One can only compare the gait of fire to that of an animal: it must first leave one place before occupying another; it moves like an amoeba and a giraffe at the same time, its neck lurching, its foot dragging) . . .

Then, while the substances consumed with method collapse, the escaping gasses are subsequently transformed into one long flight of butterflies.

▣ The Cycle of the Seasons

Tired of having restrained themselves all winter, the trees suddenly take themselves for fools. They can stand it no longer: they let loose their words—a flood, a vomiting of green. They try to bring off a complete leafing of words. Oh well, too bad! It'll arrange itself any old way! In fact, it does arrange itself! No freedom whatever in leafing . . . They fling out all kinds of words, or so they think; fling out stems to hold still more words. "Our trunks," they say, "are there to shoulder it all." They try to hide, to get lost among each other. They think they can say everything, blanket the world with assorted words: but all they are saying is "trees." They can't even hold on to the birds who fly off again, and here they are rejoicing in having produced such strange flowers! Always the same leaf, always the same way of unfolding, the same limits; leaves always symmetrical to each other, symmetrically hung! Try another leaf. —The same! Once more. —Still the same! In short, nothing can put an end to it, except this sudden realization: "There is no way out of trees by means of trees." One more fatigue, one more change of mood. "Let it all yellow and fall. Let there be silence, bareness, AUTUMN."

◨ **The Mollusk**

The mollusk is a *being . . . almost a . . . quality*. It does not need a framework; just a rampart, something like paint inside a tube.

Here nature gives up the formal presentation of plasma. But she does show her interest by sheltering it carefully, inside a jewel case whose inner surface is the more beautiful.

So it's not just a glob of spittle, but a most precious reality.

The mollusk is endowed with a powerful force for locking itself in. To be perfectly frank, it's only a muscle, a hinge, a door closure with a door.

A door closure that secreted its door. Two slightly concave doors make up its entire dwelling.

Its first and last. It lives there until after its death.

No way of getting it out alive.

In this way and with this force, the tiniest cell in man's body clings to words—and vice versa.

Sometimes another being comes along and desecrates this tomb—when it is well made—and settles there in the defunct builder's place.

The hermit crab for example.

◻ Snails

Unlike cinders (*escarbilles*) which inhabit hot ash, snails (*escargots*) are partial to moist earth. *Go on**— they move forward glued to it with their whole bodies. They carry it away, they eat it, they excrete it. It goes through them. They go through it. An interpenetration in the best of taste, tone on tone so to speak—with a passive and an active element, the passive one simultaneously bathing and nourishing the active one, which displaces itself while it feeds.

(There is something else to be said about snails. To begin with, their own moisture. Their cold blood. Their extensibility.)

It might also be said that one can hardly imagine a snail outside its shell and not moving. As soon as it rests it withdraws deep into itself. On the other hand, its modesty makes it move as soon as it shows its nakedness, reveals its vulnerable form. It no sooner exposes itself than it moves on.

During dry spells, snails retire to ditches where the presence of their bodies apparently contributes to maintaining the moisture. There, no doubt, they neighbor with other cold-blooded creatures: toads, frogs . . . But when snails come out of the ditch it is not at the same pace as the others. Their merit in going in is much greater since getting out is so much harder.

Also to be noted: though they like moist earth, they do not like places where the proportion favors water, like swamps or ponds. And certainly they prefer solid ground, provided it is rich and moist.

They are also very partial to vegetables and plants

* In English in the original.

whose leaves are green and water-laden. They know how to eat them, snipping off the tenderest parts and leaving only the veins. They really are the scourge of the salad patch.

What are they down in the ditch? Beings who enjoy it for certain of its attributes, but who have every intention of leaving it. They are one of its constituent, though wandering, elements. And what is more, down in the ditch just as in the daylight of hard paths, their shell preserves their aloofness.

It must surely be a nuisance to carry this shell around everywhere, but they do not complain and in the end are quite satisfied. How marvelous, wherever one is, to be able to go home and shut out intruders. That makes it well worth the bother.

They drivel with pride over this ability, this convenience. "How do I manage to be so sensitive, so vulnerable a creature and yet so sheltered from intruders' assaults, so securely in possession of happiness and peace of mind?" Which explains that admirable carriage.

Though at the same time so attached to the earth, so touching and slow, so progressive and so capable of detaching myself from the earth to withdraw into myself and let the world go hang—a light kick can send me rolling anywhere. Yet I am quite sure of regaining my footing and re-attaching myself to the earth, wherever fate may have sent me, and finding my pasture right there: earth, most commonplace of foods.

What happiness, what joy then, to be a snail! But they stamp the mark of that proud drivel on everything they touch. A silver wake follows after them. And perhaps points them out to the winged beaks that have a passion for them. That is the catch, the question—to be or not to be (among the vain)—the danger.

All alone, obviously the snail is very much alone. He doesn't have many friends. But he doesn't need any to be happy. He is so attached to nature, enjoys it so completely and so intimately, he is a friend of the soil he kisses with his whole body, of the leaves, and of the sky toward which he so proudly lifts his head with its sensitive eyeballs; noble, slow, wise, proud, vain, arrogant.

Let us not suggest that in this he resembles the pig. No, he does not have those silly little feet, that nervous trot. That urge, that cowardice to run away in panic. Far more resistant, more stoic. More methodical, more dignified and surely less gluttonous. Less capricious—leaving this food to fall on another; less frantic and rushed in his gluttony, less fearful of missing out on something.

Nothing is more beautiful than this way of proceeding, slowly, surely, discreetly, and at what pains, this perfect gliding with which they honor the earth! Like a long ship with a silver wake. This way of moving forward is majestic, above all if one takes into account their vulnerability, their sensitive eyeballs.

Is a snail's anger noticeable? Are there examples of it? Since no gesture expresses it, perhaps it manifests itself by a more flocculent, more rapid secretion of drivel. That drivel of pride. In that case, their anger is expressed in the same way as their pride. Thus they reassure themselves and impress the world more richly, more silverly.

The expression of their anger, as well as their pride, shines when it dries. But it also constitutes their trace and signals them to the ravisher (the predator). And is furthermore ephemeral, only lasting until the next rainfall.

So it is with all those who unrepentingly express themselves in a wholly subjective way, and only in traces, with no concern for constructing and shaping their expression like a solid building with many dimensions; more durable than themselves.

But evidently they don't feel this need. They are heroes—beings whose existence is itself a work of art, rather than artists—makers of works of art.

Here I am touching on one of the major points of the lesson they offer, which is not by the way particular to them but which they have in common with all shell-bearing creatures: this shell, a part of their being, is at the same time a work of art, a monument. It lasts far longer than they.

And that is the lesson they offer us. They are saints, making their life into a work of art—a work of art of their self-perfection. Their very secretion is produced in such a way that it creates its own form. Nothing exterior to them, to their essence, to their need is of their making. Nothing disproportionate, either, about their physique. Nothing unessential to it, required for it.

In this way they trace man's duty for him. Great thoughts spring from the heart. Perfect yourself morally and you will produce beautiful lines. Morals and rhetoric combine in the ambition and yearning of the sage.

But in what way saints? In their precise obedience to their own nature. Therefore, first know thyself. And accept yourself for what you are. In keeping with your vices.* In proportion to your size.

And what is the proper notion of man? Words and morals. Humanism.

Paris, 21 March 1936

* The original edition of 1942 reads: "En accord avec tes vues." The subsequent edition of 1949 reads: "En accord avec tes vices." I have opted for the latter.

▣ The Butterfly

When the sugar prepared in the stem rises to the bottom
of the flower, like a badly washed cup—a great event
takes place on the ground where butterflies suddenly
take off.

Because each caterpillar had its head blinded and
blackened, and its torso shrunk by the veritable explosion from which its symmetrical wings flamed—

From then on the erratic butterfly no longer alights
except by chance of route, or just about.

A flying match, its flame is not contagious. Furthermore, it arrives too late and can only acknowledge the
flowers' blooming. Never mind: in the role of lamp-
lighter, it checks the oil supply in each one, places on
top of the flower the atrophied cocoon it carries, and so
avenges its long, amorphous humiliation as a caterpillar
at the stem's foot.

Miniscule airborne sailboat abused by the wind mis-
taking it for a twice-spawned petal, it gallivants around
the garden.

▣ Moss

Patrols of vegetation once halted on stupefied rocks.
Then thousands of tiny velvet rods sat themselves down
cross-legged.

After that, ever since the apparent stiffening of the
moss and its marshals against the rock, everything in

the world—caught in inextricable confusion and fastened underneath—panics, stampedes, suffocates.

What's more, hairs have sprouted; with time, everything has grown more shadowed.

Oh, hairy preoccupations growing ever hairier! Thick rugs, in prayer when one is sitting on them, rise up today with muddled aspirations. In this way not only suffocations, but drownings occur.

Now it is becoming possible to scalp the austere and solid old rock of these terrains of saturated terrycloth, these dripping bath mats.

▣ Seashores

The sea, up to the edge of its limits, is a simple thing that repeats itself wave after wave. But in nature not even the simplest things reveal themselves without all kinds of fuss and formality, nor the most complex without undergoing some simplification. This—and also for reasons of rancor against the immensity that overwhelms him—is why man rushes to the perimeters and intersections of great things in order to define them. For at the heart of the uniform, reasoning is dangerously shaky and elusive: a mind in search of ideas should first stock up on appearances.

Where the air—plagued by the variations of its temperature and its tragic quest for influence and self-attained information on everything—does no more than superficially leaf through and dog-ear the voluminous marine tome, the other more stable element that supports us obliquely plunges into it broad earthy daggers, all the way to their rocky hilt, which remain in its thickness. Sometimes, on encountering an energetic muscle, a blade re-emerges bit by bit: that is what is called a beach.

Disoriented in the open air, yet rejected by the depths though up to a point familiar with them, this part of the expanse stretches out between the two, tawny and barren, and usually sustains nothing but a treasure of debris tirelessly collected and polished by the wrecker.

An elemental concert, more delightful and meditative for its discreetness, has been tuning up there throughout eternity for no one: but now, for the first time since its formation by the spirit of perseverance that blows from the skies acting on a limitless platitude, the wave that came harmless and blameless from afar finally has someone to talk to. But only one short word is confided to the pebbles and to the shells which appear fairly stirred by it, and the wave expires while uttering it. And all the waves to follow will also expire while uttering the same word, though at times spoken ever so slightly louder. Each wave, arriving one over the other at the orchestra, raises its collar, bares its head and states its name wherever sent. A thousand homonymic peers are thus presented on the same day in labial offerings by the prolix and prolific sea to each of her shores.

It is surely not an uncouth harangue by some Danube peasant* who comes to make himself heard in your forum, oh pebbles; no, it is the Danube itself, mixed with all the other rivers of the world after losing their direction and pretension, deeply withdrawn in bitter disillusionment, bitter except to the taste of one who would trouble to appreciate, by absorption, its most secret quality—flavor.

* Allusion to La Fontaine's fable, "Le Paysan du Danube."

In fact, it is only after the rivers' anarchic release into the deep and thickly populated commonplace of liquid matter, that the name of sea is conferred. That is why the sea will always seem absent to her own shores: taking advantage of the reciprocal separation that prevents them from communicating with each other except across her or by great detours, she probably lets each one believe it is her particular destination. In truth, she is polite to everyone, more than polite: for each of them capable of every transport, every successive conviction, she stores her infinite supply of currents at the bottom of her everlasting basin. She never goes out of bounds except a bit, she herself restrains the fury of her outbursts and, like the jellyfish she leaves for the fishermen as a miniature or sample of herself, only makes an ecstatic bow on all sides.

This is the story of Neptune's ancient mantle, that pseudo-organic pile of veils distributed evenly over three-quarters of the world. Not by the blind dagger of rocks, nor by the most penetrating storm flipping reams of pages at once, nor by the attentive eye of man—used with effort yet without control in an environment unsuited to the unstoppered orifices of the other senses, and even more disturbed by a plunging grasping hand—has this book been read, when you get to the bottom of it.

□ **Water**

Below me, always below me is water. Always with lowered eyes do I look at it. It is like the ground, like a part of the ground, a modification of the ground.

It is bright and brilliant, formless and fresh, passive

yet persistent in its one vice, gravity; disposing of extraordinary means to satisfy that vice—twisting, piercing, eroding, filtering.

This vice works from within as well: water collapses all the time, constantly sacrifices all form, tends only to humble itself, flattens itself on the ground, like a corpse, like the monks of certain orders. Always lower—that could be its motto; the opposite of excelsior.

*   *   *

One might almost say that water is mad, because of its hysterical need to obey gravity alone, a need that possesses it like an obsession.

Of course, everything in the world responds to this need, which always and everywhere must be satisfied. This cabinet, for example, proves to be terribly stubborn in its desire to stay on the ground, and if one day it found itself badly balanced, would sooner fall to pieces than run counter to that desire. But to a certain degree it teases gravity, defies it; does not give way in all its parts: its cornice, its moldings do not give in. Inherent in the cabinet is a resistence that benefits its personality and form.

LIQUID, by definition, is that which chooses to obey gravity rather than maintain its form, which rejects all form in order to obey gravity—and which loses all dignity because of that obsession, that pathological anxiety. Because of that vice—which makes it fast, flowing, or stagnant, formless or fearsome, formless *and* fearsome, piercingly fearsome in cases; devious, filtering, winding—one can do anything one wants with it, even lead water through pipes to make it spout out vertically so as to enjoy the way it collapses in droplets: a real slave.

The sun and the moon, however, are envious of this

exclusive influence, and try to take over whenever water happens to offer the opening of great expanses, and above all when in a state of least resistance—spread out in shallow puddles. Then the sun exacts an even greater tribute: forces it into a perpetual cycle, treats it like a gerbil on a wheel.

* * *

Water eludes me . . . slips between my fingers. And even so! It's not even that clean (like a lizard or a frog): it leaves traces, spots, on my hands that are quite slow to dry or have to be wiped. Water escapes me yet marks me, and there is not a thing I can do about it.

Ideologically it's the same thing: it eludes me, eludes all definition, but in my mind and on this sheet leaves traces, formless marks.

* * *

Water's instability: sensitive to the slightest change of level. Running down stairs two at a time. Playful, childishly obedient, returning as soon as called if one alters the slope on this side.

◻ **A Cut of Meat**

Each cut of meat is a kind of factory, milling and pressing blood.

Tubulures, blast furnaces, vats stand side by side with pile drivers, layers of fat.

Vapor spurts out, boiling hot. Fires dark or bright flare up.

Streams gape wide oozing gall through the slag.

And everything grows cold as night falls, death falls.

If not rust, then other chemical reactions occur at once, releasing pestilential odors.

◘ The Gymnast

Like his G, the gymnast wears a goatee and moustache almost reached by the heavy lock on his low forehead.

Molded into a jersey that makes two folds over his groin, he too, like his Y,* wears his appendage on the left.

He devastates every heart but owes it to himself to be chaste, and his only curse is BASTA!

Pinker than nature and less agile than a monkey, he leaps on the rigging, possessed by pure zeal. Then, his body stuck in the ropes, he queries the air with his head like a worm in its mound.

To wind up, he sometimes drops from the rafters like a caterpillar, but bounces back on his feet, and it is then the adulated paragon of human stupidity who salutes you.

◘ The Young Mother

Shortly after childbirth a woman's beauty is transformed.

The face often bent over the chest lengthens a bit. The eyes, attentively lowered on a nearby object, seem to wander when they look up from time to time. They re-

* Try printing a Y by hand.

veal a glance full of trust, while soliciting continuity. The arms and hands curve and strengthen. The legs which have greatly thinned and weakened are willingly seated, knees drawn up. The belly is distended, livid, still tender; the womb placidly yields to sleep, to night, to sheets.

. . . But soon upright again, this whole great body moves about hemmed in by a lanyard within easy reach streaming white linen squares, which every so often her free hand grasps, crumples, wisely fingers, to hang back or fold away depending on the result of this test.

▣ R. C. Seine N°

It is by way of a wooden staircase never waxed in thirty years—in the dust of cigarette butts stubbed at the door, among a platoon of petty, ill-mannered, derby-hatted, briefcase-clutching little clerks—that twice daily our asphyxia recurs.

A taciturn day reigns within this dilapidated stairwell where pale sawdust floats in suspension. To the sound of shoes dragged exhaustedly from stair to stair along a grimy axis, we go up like coffee beans nearing the grinding gears.

Everyone fancies he moves in a state of freedom, because an extremely simple force, not unlike gravity, obliges him to: from way inside the skies, the hand of misery turns the mill.

* * *

The exit, in fact, is not all that damaging to our form. The door which must be passed has only one hinge of flesh the size of a man—the guard who partly obstructs it: it is more like a sphincter than a grinding gear. Everybody is expulsed at once—shamefully safe and sound though deeply depressed—by bowels lubricated with floor wax, Flit and electric light. Brusquely separated one from the other by long intervals, one finds oneself in the nauseating atmosphere of a hospital for the indefinite cure of chronic flat purses, rushing at full speed through a kind of monastery-skating rink whose numerous canals intersect at right angles—where the uniform is a threadbare jacket.

*   *   *

Soon after, in every department, metal cabinets clang open from which, like ghastly fossil-birds dislodged from their habitat, folders fly down, landing heavily on the tables where they shake themselves off. A macabre investigation ensues. Oh, commercial illiteracy! The interminable celebration of your cult will now begin, to the clatter of the sacred machines.

In time everything is inscribed on multi-copy forms where the words reproduced in ever paler purples would probably dissolve in the disdain and boredom of the paper itself, were it not for the ledgers—those fortresses of sturdy blue cardboard perforated in the middle with a round peephole so that no sheet, once inserted, can hide in oblivion.

Two or three times a day, in the middle of this ceremony, the mail—multicolored, gleaming, dumb, like tropical birds—suddenly plops down in front of me, fresh from envelopes bearing a black postal kiss.

Each foundling sheet is then adopted, handed over to one of our little carrier pigeons who guides it to successive destinations until its final classification.

Certain jewels are used for these temporary harnessings: gilded corners, glowing clasps, gleaming paper clips all wait in their beggar's cups to be of service.

*   *   *

As the hour advances, the tide slowly rises in the wastebaskets. Just as it is about to overflow, noon strikes: a strident buzzer urges the immediate evacuation of the premises. No one needs to be told twice. A frantic race begins on the stairs where the two sexes, authorized to intermingle during the exodus though not during the entrance, outdo each other with their pushes and shoves.

That is when department heads take full cognizance of their superior station: *"Turba ruit or ruunt."** While they, at sacerdotal pace, allowing monks and novices to gallop by, slowly tour their domain, by privilege surrounded with frosted glass, in a setting whose embalming virtues are arrogance, poor taste, gossip. Once inside the cloakroom where gloves, walking sticks, silk scarves are not uncommonly found, they defrock themselves of their habitual grimace and transform themselves into true men of the world.

◻ Lemeunier's Restaurant
Rue de La Chaussée D'Antin

Nothing is more moving than the spectacle inside that enormous restaurant, Lemeunier's on the rue de la Chaussée d'Antin, provided by the horde of clerks and salesgirls who lunch there daily.

Light and music are dispensed with the prodigality of

* Classical example of the collective noun taking singular or plural verb, but a mob rushing all the same.

dreams. Bevelled mirrors, gilded moldings everywhere. One enters past green plants through a darker passage, against whose walls a few clients are already tightly installed, which leads to a room of huge proportions with a number of wooden balconies forming the figure eight. There you are assailed by billows of warm odors, clattering cutlery and dishes, shouting waitresses and the din of conversations.

It is a grandiose composition worthy of Veronese in its magnitude of ambition and dimensions, but which really should be painted in the style of Manet's famous *Bar*.

The dominant figures without a doubt are first of all the musicians up at the crossing of the eight; then the cashiers seated high behind their registers, their pastel, obligatorily well-filled blouses fully revealed; lastly, those pitiful caricatures of head waiters circulating with relative ease, but at times forced into working as fast as the waitresses, not because the diners (hardly accustomed to making demands) are impatient, but because of the fever of a professional zeal heightened by the uncertainty of employment in the current state of supply and demand on the job market.

Oh, world of tastelessness and twaddle! Here you attain your perfection! Here the mindless young daily ape the noisy frivolity that the bourgeois allows himself a few times a year, when papa-moneybags or mama-klepto come into some unexpected windfall and want to impress their neighbors *comme it faut*.

All dolled up, like their country cousins on Sundays only, these young clerks and their girlfriends dig in with delight and good conscience every day. Everybody clings to his plate like the hermit crab to its shell, while the whirling rhythm of a Viennese waltz rises above the clinking of the crockery shells to quicken hearts and stomachs.

As in an enchanted grotto, I see them laugh and speak but do not hear them. Young salesman, it is in this throng of your peers that you must talk to your companion and discover your heart. Oh secrets, it is here that you will be exchanged!

Creamy layered desserts piled daringly high—served in bowls of mysterious metal, handsomely footed but rapidly washed and always warm, alas—allow the diners who chose to have them displayed, to manifest more effectively than by other signs their deep feelings. For one, it is enthusiasm generated by the splendidly curved typist at his side, for whom he would not hesitate to commit a thousand equally costly follies; for another, it is the desire to exhibit a well-bred frugality (he started with a very modest appetizer) coupled with a promising taste for delicacies; for others, it is a way of expressing aristocratic distaste for anything in this world that hasn't a touch of magic; still others, by the way they eat, reveal a long-standing habit and surfeit of luxury.

Meanwhile, thousands of blond crumbs and pink blotches appear on the scattered or spread linen.

A little later, cigarette lighters take the leading role, according to the striking device or manner of handling; while the ladies, raising their arms in such a way that their armpits reveal each personal style of wearing perspiration's badges, rearrange their hair or toot their lipstick tubes.

This is the moment—amid the increasing tumult of chairs scraping, napkins snapping, crumbs crushing— for the final ritual in this unique ceremony. Moving their sweetly aproned tummies close to each guest in turn, a notebook in their pocket, a pencil stub in their hair, the waitresses apply themselves from memory to a rapid calculation. It is then that vanity is punished and modesty rewarded. Coins and bills change hands across the table, as though everybody were cashing in his chips.

Fomented by the waitresses during the final dinner servings, a general uprising of furniture is slowly instigated and behind closed doors accomplished, permitting the damp chores of cleaning to be undertaken at once and finished without hindrance.

It is only then that the working girls, one by one jingling the few coins in their pockets, hearts swollen with the thought of a child raised in the country or looked after by a neighbor, take apathetic leave of these extinguished rooms, while from the sidewalk opposite, the man waiting for them sees nothing but a vast menagerie of chairs and tables, ears cocked, stacked to contemplate the empty street dumbly and intently.

▣ Notes Toward a Shell

A shell is a little thing, but I can make it look bigger by replacing it where I found it, on the vast expanse of sand. For if I take a handful of sand and observe what little remains in my hand after most of it has run out between my fingers, if I observe a few grains, then each grain individually, at that moment none of the grains seems small to me any longer, and soon the shell itself —this oyster shell or limpet or razor clam—will appear to be an enormous monument, both colossal and intri-

cate, like the temples of Angkor, or the church of Saint-
Maclou, or the Pyramids, and with a meaning far
stranger than these unquestioned works of man.

If I then stop to think that this shell, which a tongue
of the sea can cover up, is inhabited by an animal, and
if I add an animal to this shell by imagining it back
under a few inches of water, you can well understand
how much greater, more intense my impression becomes,
and how different from the impression that can be produced by even the most remarkable of the monuments
I just mentioned.

* * *

Man's monuments resemble the parts of his skeleton,
or of any skeleton, with its big fleshless bones; they
evoke no habitant of their size. What emerges from the
greatest cathedrals is merely a formless throng of ants,
and even the most sumptuous villas or palaces, made
for only one man, are still more like bee hives or
many-chambered ant hills than shells. When the lord
leaves his manor he is certainly less impressive than the
hermit crab exposing his monstrous claw at the mouth
of the superb cone that houses him.

It may amuse me to think of Rome or Nîmes as a
scattered skeleton—here a tibia, there the skull of a once
living city, a once living citizen—but then I am obliged
to imagine an enormous colossus of flesh and blood,
which really has no bearing on what can be reasonably
inferred from what we were taught, even with the aid
of such expressions in the singular as The Roman People, The Persian Host.

How I would like someone, some day, to show me
that such a colossus really existed; someone to support
in some way my shaky belief in that phantasmic and

singularly abstract vision! To be allowed to touch his
cheeks, feel the shape of his arm, and the way it hung
at his side.

All this the shell gives us: we are in full possession
of it; we are never outside of nature; the mollusk and
the crustacean are truly there. Which produces a kind
of uneasiness that augments our pleasure.

*   *   *

I wish that—instead of those enormous monuments
which only testify to the grotesque exaggeration of his
imagination and his body (or his revolting social and
convivial mores), instead of those statues scaled to him
or slightly larger (I am thinking of Michaelangelo's
David) which are only simple representations—man
sculpted some kind of niches or shells to his proportion,
something very different from the mollusk form yet
similarly proportioned (in this respect I find African
huts fairly satisfactory); that man used his skill to
create over generations a dwelling not much larger than
his body; that all his imagination and reason went into it;
that he used his genius for adaptation, not disproportion—or at least that his genius recognized the limits of
the body that contains it.

I do not even admire men like Pharaoh who used a
multitude to erect monuments to only one; I would
rather he had used this multitude for a work no larger
or not much larger than his own body, or—which would
have been even worthier—that he proved his superiority
to other men by the nature of his own work.

In this sense I most admire a few restrained writers
and musicians—Bach, Rameau, Malherbe, Horace, Mallarmé—and writers most of all, because their monument
is made of the genuine secretion common to the human
mollusk, the thing most proportioned and suited to his

body, yet as utterly different from his form as can be imagined: I mean WORDS.

Oh Louvre of the written word, which can perhaps, after the race has vanished, be inhabited by other dwellers, apes for example, or birds, or some superior being, just as the crustacean replaces the mollusk in the hermit crab.

And then, at the end of the whole animal kingdom, air and tiny grains of sand slowly seep into it, while on the ground it goes on sparkling and eroding, and disintegrates brilliantly. Oh sterile, immaterial dust, oh brilliant debris, though endlessly rolled and flattened between laminators of air and water, AT LAST!—there is *no one* left, no one to refashion the sand, not even into glass, and IT IS THE END!

◻ **The Three Shops**

Near the Place Maubert, where I wait early every morning for the bus, three shops stand side by side: a jewelry shop, a coal and wood shop, a butcher shop. Examining them one by one, I seem to notice differences of behavior between coal, logs, cuts of meat.

Let us not linger too long over metals, which are only the result of man's violent or divisive action on various kinds of mud or particular agglomerates that had no such intentions of their own; nor on precious stones whose very rarity warrants only a few well chosen words in an equitably composed discourse on nature.

As to meat, a quavering at the sight of it, a kind of horror or sympathy, forces upon me the greatest discretion. Moreover, when freshly cut, a veil of steam or smoke conceals it from the very eyes that would prove their cynicism in the strict sense of the word. I will have said all that I can say if for one moment I have drawn attention to its *panting* appearance.

On the other hand, the contemplation of wood and coal is a source of pleasures as instant as they are sober and certain, which I would be pleased to share. One would probably need many pages for this, whereas I have only half of one. This is why I shall limit myself to proposing the following subjects for meditation:

1. TIME SPENT IN VECTORS ALWAYS AVENGES ITSELF, IN DEATH.

2. BROWN, BECAUSE BROWN LIES BETWEEN GREEN AND BLACK ON THE WAY TO CARBONIZATION, THE DESTINY OF WOOD STILL HOLDS—THOUGH MINIMALLY—THE POSSIBILITY OF ACTION, MEANING ERROR, BLUNDER, AND EVERY POSSIBLE MISUNDERSTANDING.

◩ Fauna and Flora

Fauna moves, while flora unfolds to the eye.

The soil is directly in charge of a whole order of living things.

Their place in the world is assured, as is their badge of honor by seniority.

Unlike their vagrant brothers, they are not adjuncts to the world, intruders in the ground. They do not wander around in search of a place to die, since the earth, like others, meticulously absorbs their remains.

For them, no problems of food and lodging, no cannibalism; no terrors, wild escapades, cruelties, sighs, cries or words. They are not parties to upheaval, madness or murder.

From their first appearance in the light of day, they have a window on the street or road. Unconcerned about their neighbors, they do not merge one with the other by means of ingestion. They do not emerge one from the other by means of gestation. They die of dehydration and prostration under the sun, or rather collapse on the spot; rarely from contamination. No area of the body so sensitive that if pierced it can cause the death of the whole individual. But relatively more sensitive to climate and conditions of existence.

They are not . . . They are not . . .
Their hell is of a different kind.

They have no voice. They are nearly paralytic. They can only draw attention with their poses. They seem to know nothing about the agonies of non-justification. In any event, they could never escape this obsession by running away, or believe they are escaping it in the drunkenness of speed. There is no movement in them besides extension. No gesture, no thought, no desire perhaps, no intuition that does not lead to a monstrous increment of their bodies, an irremediable *excrescence.*

Or rather, and even worse, nothing accidentally monstrous: despite all their efforts "to express themselves," they only manage to repeat a million times over the same expression, the same leaf. In the spring, when tired of restraining themselves and no longer able to hold out, they let loose a flood, a vomiting of green, and think they are humming a tuneful hymn, coming out of themselves, spreading out over all of nature, embracing it— they are still only producing in thousands of copies the same note, the same word, the same leaf.

There is no way out for trees by the means of trees.

* * *

"They express themselves only through their poses."

No gestures, they simply multiply their arms, their hands, their fingers—like buddhas. In this idle way of theirs they go to the end of their thoughts. All they are is the will for expression. They hide nothing, keep no idea secret; they open up completely, sincerely, unreservedly.

Idle creatures, they pass the time complicating their own form, perfecting their own body in terms of the greatest analytical complication. Wherever they grow, however hidden they are, their only activity is the accomplishment of their expression: they prepare themselves, wait for someone to come and read them.

All they have available to draw attention are poses, lines, and once in a while an exceptional signal, an extraordinary appeal to the eyes and the nose in the form of luminous, fragrant blisters or swellings called flowers, which may well be lesions.

This modification of the perpetual leaf certainly means something.

* * *

The time of plants: they always seem fixed, immobile. One ignores them for a few days, a week, and their pose is all the sharper, their limbs have multiplied. Their identity raises no doubts, yet their form goes on elaborating itself.

* * *

The beauty of wilting flowers: the petals curl as though touched by fire, which in fact is what happens— dehydration. They curl up to reveal the seeds, deciding to offer them their chance, a clear field. That is when nature confronts the flower, forces it to open up and step aside: it contracts, twists, recoils, and allows the seed that emerged from it, was prepared by it, to triumph.

* * *

The time of plants is conditioned by their space, the space they gradually occupy filling in a canvas doubtless determined forevermore. Once finished, weariness overtakes them, and it is the drama of a certain season.

Like the development of crystals: a will to formation, and the impossibility of forming *any other way*.

* * *

Among living things it is possible to distinguish between those in which a force, other than the movement to grow, permits them to move all or parts of their body, and move in their own way anywhere—and those in which there is no movement except extension.

Once freed from the obligation to grow, the first *express themselves* in many ways: in their concerns over lodging, food, protection, and even in certain games when they finally have the time.

The second, who know nothing of these pressing needs, cannot be said to have no intentions or desires besides growth, but whatever desire for expression they do have remains impotent except to develop their body, as though each of our desires cost us the future responsibility of feeding and maintaining an additional member. Infernal multiplication of substance with the birth of each idea! Each desire for escape weighs me down by one more link!

* * *

The plant is an analysis enacted, a unique dialectic in space. Progress by division of the preceding act. Animal expression is oral, or mimed by gestures that erase each other. Plant expression is written, once and for all. No way of retracting, no repenting possible: correcting means adding. A text written and *published* is corrected by appendices, and still more appendices. It should be added, however, that they do not divide to infinity. In each there is a limit.

Each of their gestures not only leaves a trace, as with man and his writings, but also a presence, an irrevocable birth, *not detached from them.*

*   *   *

Their poses or "tableaux vivants": mute entreaties, supplications, unshakable calm, triumphs.

*   *   *

It is said that cripples, amputees, notice a prodigious development of their faculties. So with plants: their immobility accounts for their self-perfection, their complexity, their gorgeous decorations, their lush fruits.

*   *   *

None of their gestures has any effect outside themselves.

*   *   *

The infinite variety of sentiments born of desire in immobility has given rise to the infinite variety of their forms.

*   *   *

A body of the most excessively complex laws (pure chance, in other words) presides over the birth and distribution of plants across the globe.

The law of *undetermined determinants.*

*   *   *

Plants at night.

The exhalation of carbon dioxide resulting from photosynthesis, like a sigh of satisfaction that goes on for hours; like the lowest note on a stringed instrument, bowed all the way, that vibrates to the limits of music, of pure sound, of silence.

* * *

THOUGH THE VEGETAL BEING WOULD RATHER BE DE-FINED BY ITS CONTOURS AND FORMS, I SHALL FIRST PAY TRIBUTE TO A VIRTUE OF ITS SUBSTANCE: THAT OF BEING ABLE TO ACHIEVE ITS SYNTHESIS SOLELY AT THE EX-PENSE OF ITS INORGANIC ENVIRONMENT. THE WORLD AROUND IT IS ONLY A MINE FROM WHICH THE PRECIOUS GREEN VEIN EXTRACTS THE WHEREWITHAL TO CONTINUE MAKING ITS PROTOPLASM—FROM THE AIR, THROUGH THE PHOTOSYNTHESIS OF ITS LEAVES; FROM THE EARTH, THROUGH THE ABSORBENCY OF ITS ROOTS WHICH AS-SIMILATE MINERALS. WHENCE THE ESSENTIAL QUALITY OF THIS BEING, LIBERATED FROM ALL CONCERNS OF FOOD OR LODGING BY THE SURROUNDING PRESENCE OF AN INFINITE SUPPLY OF NOURISHMENT: *Immobility*.

◻ Vegetation

Rain is not the only hyphen between sky and earth; there is another, less intermittent and better made, whose fabric the wind cannot carry off no matter how hard it blows. If during a certain season the wind manages to break off a bit, which it then tries to diminish in its maelstrom, one sees in the final analysis that it has de-stroyed nothing at all.

On closer examination, one finds oneself at one of the innumerable doors to an immense laboratory bristling with multiform hydraulic systems, all far more complicated than the rain's simple columns, and of singular perfection: retorts, filters, siphons, alembics, all in one.

These are the devices that rain encounters first, before it reaches the ground. They catch it in a number of small bowls, placed all around at various levels, which empty one into the other, down to the ones on the lowest level, which finally moisten the earth directly.

Thus in their own way they retard the downpour, and long after it has subsided hold onto its fluid and its benefit to the soil. They alone have the power to make the rain's forms glimmer in the sunlight; in other words, to display from a viewpoint of joy the reasons accepted as readily by religion as they were precipitously formulated by sadness. Curious occupation, enigmatic characters.

They grow taller as the rain falls, but with greater regularity, discretion, and even when the rain stops falling, by a kind of momentum. Later on one still finds water in the swellings they form and bear with blushing ostentation, called their fruits.

Such, it would seem, is the function of this type of three-dimensional tapestry which has been named vegetation for its other characteristics, and particularly for the kind of life it leads . . . But first, I wanted to stress this point: although the ability to accomplish their own synthesis and to reproduce without being asked (even between the paving stones of the Sorbonne) relates plants to animals, which is to say to all kinds of vagabonds, nonetheless, in many places where they settle they create a fabric, and that fabric provides the world with one of its pillars.

◙ The Pebble

A pebble is not an easy thing to define.

If one is satisfied with a simple description, one can start out by saying it is a form or state of stone between rock and gravel.

But this remark already implies a notion of stone that has to be justified. On this subject let me not be reproached for going even farther back than the Flood.

*   *   *

All rocks are offsprings through fission of the same enormous forebear. All one can say about this fabulous body is that once outside of limbo it did not remain standing.

When reason gets to it, it is already amorphous and sprawling in the doughy heavings of the death agony. Awakening for the baptism of a hero of the world's grandeur, reason discovers instead the ghastly trough of a death bed.

Let the reader not rush through this, but take the time to admire—instead of dense funereal expressions—the grandeur and glory of a truth that has managed, whatever the degree, to render these expressions transparent yet not obscure itself completely.

This is how, on a planet already drab and cold, the sun presently shines. There is no flaming satellite to dissemble this fact any longer. All glory and all existence, everything that grants vision and vitality, the source of all objective reality has gone over to the sun. The heroes it engendered who gravitated around it have let themselves be eclipsed. But in order for the truth—whose glory they relinquish in behalf of its very source—

to retain an audience and objects, already dead or about to be, they nonetheless continue to orbit around it and serve as spectators.

One can imagine that such a sacrifice—the expulsion of life from natures once glorious and ardent—was not accomplished without some dramatic inner upheavals. There you have the origin of the gray chaos of the Earth, our humble and magnificent abode.

And so, after a period of twists and turns, like a sleeping body thrashing under blankets, our hero, subdued (by his consciousness) as though by a gigantic straitjacket, no longer felt anything but intimate explosions, less and less frequent, with shattering effects on a mantle that grew heavier and colder.

Deceased hero and chaotic earth are nowadays confused.

*   *   *

The history of this body—having once and for all lost the capacity of being aroused in addition to that of recasting itself into a total entity—ever since the slow catastrophe of cooling, will be no more than a history of perpetual disintegration. But at this very moment other things happen: with grandeur dead, life at once makes clear that the two have nothing in common. At once, in countless ways.

Such is the globe's appearance today. The severed cadaver of the being that was once the world's grandeur now serves merely as a background for the life of millions of beings infinitely smaller and more ephemeral. In places, their crowding is so dense it completely hides the sacred skeleton that was once their sole support. And it is only the infinite number of their corpses, having succeeded from that time in imitating the consistency of stone with what is called organic soil, that permits them of late to reproduce without owing any-thing to the rock.

Then too the liquid element, whose origin is perhaps as ancient as that of the element under discussion, having collected over greater and lesser areas, covers it, rubs it, and by repeated abrasion encourages its erosion.

I shall now describe some of the forms that stone, currently scattered and humbled by the world, offers for our examination.

* * *

The largest fragments—slabs almost invisible under the entwining plants that cling to them as much for re-ligious as for other motives—make up the global skele-ton.

These are veritable temples: not constructions arbi-trarily raised above the ground, but the serene remains of the ancient hero who was really in the world not long ago.

Given to imagining great things amid the shadows and scents of the forests which sometimes cover these mys-terious blocks, man by thought alone infers their con-tinued existence beneath him.

In these same places, numerous smaller blocks attract his attention. Sprinkled in the underbrush by Time are odd-sized stonecrumbs, rolled between the dirty fingers of that god.

Ever since the explosion of their enormous forebear and their trajectory into the skies felled beyond redress, the rocks have kept silent.

Invaded and fractured by germination, like a man who has stopped shaving, furrowed and filled with loose earth, none of them, now incapable of any reaction at all, makes a sound any longer.

Their faces, their bodies are lined. Naiveté draws

close and settles in the wrinkles of experience. Roses sit on their gray knees and launch their naïve diatribe against them. And they let them, they whose disastrous hail once lit up forests, whose duration in stupor and resignation is eternal.

They laugh to see around them so many generations of flowers born and condemned, whose coloring, whatever one says, is hardly more vivid than theirs, a pink as pale as their gray. They think (like statues, not bothering to say it) that these hues were borrowed from the rays of the setting sun, rays donned by the skies every evening in memory of a far brighter fire—that famous cataclysm during which they were hurled violently into the air and enjoyed an hour of stupendous freedom brought to an end by that formidable crash. Nearby, at the rocky knees of the giants watching from her shores the foaming labors of their fallen wives, the sea endlessly tears off blocks which she keeps, hugs, cradles, dandles in her arms; sifts, kneads, flattens, smoothes against her body; or leaves in a corner of her mouth like a Jordan almond, which she later takes out and places on some gentle sloping shore within easy reach of her already sizable collection, with the idea of picking it up soon again and caring for it even more affectionately, even more passionately.

Meanwhile, the wind blows making the sand whirl. And if one of these particles—last and smallest form of the object under consideration—happens to enter our eyes, it is in this way—its own blinding way—that stone punishes and terminates our contemplation.

Nature thus closes our eyes when it comes time to ask of memory whether the information gathered there by prolonged contemplation has not already provided it with a few principles.

*   *   *

To the mind in search of ideas which has first been nourished on such appearances, nature in terms of stone will ultimately appear, perhaps too simplistically—like a watch whose mechanism consists of wheels turning at different speeds though run by the same motor.

To die and live again, plants, animals, gases and liquids move more or less rapidly. The great wheel of stone seems to us practically, and even theoretically, immobile; we can only imagine a portion of its slowly disintegrating phase.

So that contrary to popular opinion, which makes stone in man's eyes a symbol of durability and impassiveness, one might say that stone, which does not regenerate, is in fact the only thing in nature that constantly dies.

And so when life, through the mouths of beings who successively and briefly get a taste of it, pretends to envy the indestructible solidity of its setting, the truth is it contributes to the continual disintegration of that setting. It is this unity of action that life finds so dramatic: it mistakenly believes that its foundation may one day fail it, while believing itself to be eternally renewable. Placed in a setting that has given up being moved, and dreams only of falling into ruin, life becomes nervous and agitated about knowing only how to renew.

At times stone itself seems agitated. This is in its final stages when, as pebble, gravel, sand, dust, it can no longer play its part as container or supporter of living things. Cut off from the original block, it rolls, flies, demands a place on the surface, and all of life retreats from the drab expanses where the frenzy of despair alternately scatters and reassembles it.

Finally, I would like to mention a very important principle, namely, that all forms of stone, all of which represent some stage of its evolution, exist simulta-

neously in the world. No generations, no vanished races
here. Temples, Demigods, Wonders of the World, Mam-
moths, Heroes, Ancestors, live in daily contact with their
grandchildren. Any man in his own garden can touch
all the fully fleshed potentials of this world. There is no
conception: everything exists. Or rather, as in paradise,
all conception exists.

*   *   *

If I now wish to examine a specific type of stone with
greater attention, its perfection of form and the fact that
I can hold it, roll it around in my hand, makes me
choose the pebble.

Furthermore, the pebble is stone at precisely that
stage when it reaches the age of the person, the individual, in other words, the age of speech.

Compared to the rocky ledge from which it is directly
descended, it is stone already fragmented and polished
into many nearly similar individuals. Compared to the
finest gravel, one can say that because of where it is
found and because not even man puts it to practical use,
the pebble is stone still wild, or at least not domesticated.

For the remaining days without meaning in a world
with no practical order, let us profit from its virtues.

*   *   *

Brought one day by one of the tide's countless wagons
which seem to unload their useless cargo just for the
sound of it, each pebble rests on a pile of its past and
future forms.

Not far from places where a layer of loam still covers
its enormous forebears, beneath the rocky ledge where
its parents' love act still goes on, the pebble takes up
residence on ground formed by their seed, where the
bulldozing sea seeks it and loses it.

But these places to which the sea generally relegates it are the least suited to granting recognition. Whole populations lie there known only to the expanse, each pebble considering itself lost because it is unnumbered and sees only blind forces taking note of it.

In fact, wherever such flocks lie down they all but cover the ground completely, and their backs form a floor as awkward for the foot as for the mind.

No birds. Here and there a few blades of grass between the pebbles. Lizards scramble over them indifferently. Grasshoppers measure themselves rather than the pebbles with their leaps. Every now and again, a man distractedly tosses one far out.

But these objects of scant value, lost without order in a solitude broken by dune grass, seaweed, old corks and other debris of human provisions—imperturbable amid the greatest upheavals of the atmosphere—are mute spectators of these forces that run blindly after anything and for no reason until exhausted.

Rooted nowhere, they remain in their haphazard spot on the expanse. A wind strong enough to uproot a tree or knock down a building can not displace a pebble. But since it does raise up dust, the whirlwind sometimes ferrets one of these landmarks of chance out of their haphazard places, for centuries under the opaque and temporal bed of sand.

*   *   *

Water on the other hand, which makes everything slippery and spreads its fluidity to whatever it can encompass, sometimes manages to seduce these forms and carry them off. For the pebble remembers it was born of the thrusts of these formless monsters against the equally formless monster of stone.

And since its individuality can only be accomplished

by repeated application of liquid, it remains by definition forever amenable to it.

Lackluster on the ground, as day is lackluster compared to night, the moment the wave takes hold of it, it
starts to shine. And though the wave works only superficially, barely penetrating the very fine, hard-packed
agglomerate, the very thin though active adherence of
the liquid causes a noticeable modification of its surface.
As though the water were repolishing it, thus assuaging
the wounds of their earlier embraces. Then for a moment, the pebble's exterior resembles its interior; all
over its body it has the sheen of youth.

Its perfect form is equally comfortable in either environment, remaining imperturbable in the sea's confusion. The pebble simply comes out of it a bit smaller,
but intact, and just as *great* since its proportions in no
way depend on its volume.

Once out of the water it dries immediately. Which is
to say that despite the monstrous efforts to which it was
subjected, no trace of liquid can remain on its surface;
the pebble with no effort does away with it.

In short, smaller from day to day but always sure of
its form; blind, solid and dry within; its nature does not
allow it to become muddled by the waves, merely reduced. So that when vanquished it finally becomes sand,
water can still not penetrate it as it penetrates dust.
Keeping all traces except those of liquid, which limits
itself to trying to erase all other traces, it lets the whole
sea filter through, which disappears into its depths without in any way being able to make mud out of it.

*   *   *

I shall say no more, for this idea of signs disappear-
ing makes me reflect on the faults of a style that relies
too much on words.

Only too happy to have chosen for these beginnings *the pebble:* for a man of wit cannot fail to be amused, and also moved, when my critics say: "Having undertaken to write a description of stone, he got buried under it."

II

from Methods*

* LE GRAND RECUEIL, vol. II, *Méthodes*, Paris, Gallimard, 1961.

◘ My Creative Method

Sidi-Madani,
Thursday, December 18, 1947

It may well be that I am not very intelligent; in any case ideas are not my forte. I have always been disappointed by them. The most well-founded opinions, the most harmonious (best constructed) philosophic systems have always seemed to me utterly precarious, caused in me a certain queasiness, an uneasiness, an unpleasant feeling of instability. I haven't the slightest confidence in the statements I come out with during a discussion. Contradictory remarks made by others seem to me just as valid, or let us say for the sake of precision, neither more nor less valid. I am easily convinced, easily dissuaded. And when I say convinced, I mean if not of some truth, then at least of the fragility of my own opinion. What is more, the validity of ideas most often seems to me in inverse proportion to the fervor with which they were expounded. The tone of conviction (and even sincerity) is assumed, it seems to me, as much to convince oneself as to convince one's interlocutor, and even more perhaps *to replace* conviction; to replace, in a sense, the truth missing from the statements made. This is something I feel very keenly.

Therefore ideas as such seem to me what I am least fit for, and they interest me little. You may well reply that right now we are dealing with an idea (an opinion) . . . However, ideas, opinions, strike me as determined in each of us by something quite different from free will or judgment. I don't know anything more subjective, more epiphenomenal. I really don't understand how one can be proud of them, and what I find intolerable is that one tries to impose them on others. Passing off one's opinion as objectively valid, or valid in the absolute, seems to me as absurd as maintaining, for example, that blond curly hair is *truer* than straight black hair, that the song of the nightingale is closer to the truth than the neighing of a horse. (On the other hand, I am rather inclined to formulizing and may have a talent for it. "What you mean to say is . . ." and I usually gain the agreement of the person who used the formula I proposed. Is that a writer's talent? Could be.)

In the case of what I would call observations, or let us say, experimental ideas, the situation is a bit different. I have always thought it desirable to agree, if not on opinions, at least on well established facts, and if that still sounds too pretentious, then at least on a few solid definitions.

Given such inclinations (distaste for ideas, taste for definitions), it may perhaps be natural that I devote myself first to cataloguing and defining objects in the external world, and among them, the ones that constitute the familiar universe of our culture, our time. "But," one can protest, "why begin again what has already been done repeatedly, and has been firmly established in dictionaries and encyclopedias?" "How is it then," I will reply, "that there is more than one dictionary and encyclopedia in the same language during the same period, and yet their definitions of the same objects are not identical? Even more, how is it that what one finds there seems to be more a definition of words than of things? Why is it that I have this—to be honest, somewhat silly—impression? Why is there this difference, this unthinkable margin between the definition of a word and the description of the thing designated by the word? Why is it that dictionary definitions seem to be so woefully lacking in concreteness, and descriptions (in novels or poems, for example) so incomplete (or else too specific and detailed), so arbitrary, so capricious? Couldn't one imagine some kind of writing (brand new) which, placing itself more or less between the two (definition and description), would borrow from the former its infallibility, its indubitability, and its brevity; and from the latter, its respect for the sensory aspect of things . . ."

Sidi-Madani
Saturday, December 27 (1)

1

If ideas disappoint me, give me no pleasure, it is because I offer them my approval too easily, seeing how they solicit it, are only made for that. Ideas seek my approval, demand it, and it is only too easy for me to offer it; this offering, this consent, produces no pleasure in me but rather a kind of queasiness, a nausea. On the other hand, objects, landscapes, events, individuals of the external world give me much pleasure. They win my trust. For the simple reason that they don't need it. Their concrete presence and evidence, their density, their three dimensions, their palpable undeniable aspect, their existence—much more certain than my own, their way of implying: "this doesn't get invented (it gets discovered)"; their way of expressing: "this is beautiful because I wouldn't have invented it, I couldn't have"—all this is my sole justification for existence, or more precisely, *my pretext;* and *the variety of things is what really constructs me.* What I mean is this: their variety constructs me, permits me to exist even in silence. Like the locus around which they exist. But in relation to only one of these things, with regard to each one in particular, *if I consider no more than one,* I disappear; it annihilates me. And if it is only my pretext, my justification for existence, if indeed I must exist, if my existence begins with it, then that will only be, can only be, through some creation of mine about it.

What creation? The *text*.

And to start with, how does the idea for such a creation come to me, how did I gain an idea of it, how do I conceive of it?

Through works of art (literature).

Sidi-Madani,
Saturday, December 27 (2)

2

Imitation of the heroes of art. (Exemplary existences. Distaste for cheap concessions. Nevertheless, awareness of having to stay between the two. Proper measure. Proper balance.) Love of glory. Love of heroes (and poets) with a passion. I love my old school books (Selected Readings). Latin writers.

What I conceive of as a work of art: that which modifies, alters, changes something in the language. Which is something besides those warrior heroes!

This is *another* reality, *another* external world, which also gives me pleasure instead of seeking my approval (shocking aspect, giving rise to artistic innovations. Difference between an artistic innovation and a paradox); which is also a justification for my existence, and whose variety also constructs me (constructs me as an *amateur*, a lover of poems).

Yet here too, *each one of them* rejects me, erases (effaces) me, annihilates me. I have to exist. There has to be a creation on my part concerning them (different, original).

Here then is the kind of creation vis-à-vis the external world that I quite naturally conceive of: *a creation of an artistic, literary nature.*

3

As one can see, I am returning to my distaste for ideas and my taste for definitions.

What I shall attempt then is in the nature of a definition-description-literary art work.

4

It would seem that I can do it. How is that? Why?

What is this thing, talent?

Sidi-Madanı,
Saturday, December 27, 1947 (3)

I started out (really and truly*) by saying that I would never be able to explain myself. How is it I no longer stick to it (that position)?

Well no, really, now I don't think it at all impossible dishonorable, foolish, self-deceiving or grotesque (arro gant) to try to explain myself.

On the contrary, I think it's very nice (that I be asked to do so) and would now think it a little silly to reply by a haughty refusal out of principle. That is what would strike me as foolish, self-deceptive and grotesque. It is

---

* First line of the first piece I published: "Please excuse the apparent flaw in our relationship. I will never be able to explain myself." (*Douze Petits Ecrits*, 1926) [Author's note.]

less foolish to risk ridicule than to refuse to expose oneself out of principle. There's little chance of escaping
it no matter how. . . !

What has changed then?

What has changed is my existence in relation to others,
is that a work exists and has been talked about. It has
been set down, has set itself down as a separate existence,
and so has my "personality" in a sense. Here then these
things: my work, my personality; I can now consider
them as something quite apart, and can listen to (reply
to) the objections they raise against the explanations
made about them. I must correct those false interpretations (or definitions).

For the most part, the explanations of my work and of
myself have been more philosophical (metaphysical)
than esthetic or, more precisely, literary (technical). It
is this philosophic image, to begin with, that I would
gladly touch up a bit.

Nothing is more surprising (to me) than this interest
philosophers take in me; for truly, I am not intelligent,
ideas are not my concern, etc. But after all . . .

Sidi-Madani,
Saturday, December 27 (4)

. . . I am lazy, and as you see, even this text—I am
convinced that I don't really have to feed it original or
new ideas, fully fleeced, progressing in numerical order,
varied, coherent, etc. (theory of clouds).

In order to turn out well, I am convinced it is enough
not to fuss too much over it. First (and foremost) I
must not write too much, just a little each day and just
as it comes, without forcing, any old way. Then, work it

somehow into a literary object—somewhat original, somewhat different, humorously erudite, cut up in my own way, clumsy in my own way—that can stand on its own (and there's only one way of doing that: get rid of explanations).

And that, let me tell you, will really hold up. It will be a little thing made of style.

Enough for today!

Sidi-Madani,
Sunday, December 28, 1947

What am I talking about? Well, if I have made myself clear, about creating literary objects which are most likely I won't say to last, but steadily oppose (*object*-ify, affirm themselves as objects) the spirit of each generation; which will remain interesting to it (since each generation will always be interested in external objects); which will remain at its disposal, at the disposal of its desire and taste for the concrete, for opposable (mute) evidence, or for the representative (or presentative).

I am talking about objects of human origin, made especially for man (by man), which attain the exteriority and complexity, in addition to the presence and evidence, of natural objects. But which should be more moving, if possible, than natural objects because they are human; more decisive, more capable of gaining approval.

But to achieve that, must they—as one might suppose—be more abstract than concrete? That is the question . . . (Completely exhausted by the prefect's visit; couldn't get any farther . . .)

Sidi-Madani,
Monday, December 29, 1947

(Today, it was the absence of mail and our resulting anxiety that prevented me . . . I decided to call Paris via radio and now all is well!)

What I intend to formulate, then, are description-definition-literary art works, that is, definitions which—instead of referring (as in the case of a particular plant) to such and such a classification previously learned (accepted), or to a branch of human knowledge assumed to be known (but generally unknown)—refer, if not entirely to total ignorance, at least to common, habitual and elementary knowledge; definitions which establish uncommon relationships, break up ordinary classifications, and thereby make themselves more incisive, more striking, and more pleasing as well.

At the same time, the characteristics of the object selected for explanation will be preferably those neglected until now. If in this way we succeed in communicating our authentic impression and our naïve childlike classification of things, we shall have renewed the world of objects (subjects for literary works of art). And since there is a good chance that, however subjective and eccentric it may be, our childlike impression will nevertheless relate to the impression of minds and sensibilities of today and the future, we shall be understood, thanked and admired.

But to make them more striking and appealing, must we lean toward the abstraction of those characteristics? Here again the question comes up. Well then, at this point, and to a large degree, the answer would be *yes.* (To be developed.)

However, let's see what dictionaries we have at our disposal.

On the one hand there is the *Larousse* (or the *Encyclopédie Larousse*).

On the other, *Littré*.

The difference between them is meaningful. And our preference for one over the other, the fact that we use one rather than the other, is equally meaningful.

(Question of vocabulary to be discussed here, thoroughly.)

As to syntax, prosody and, in a larger sense, rhetoric, here again their renewal will be instinctive and uninhibited (though prudent, and solely concerned with the result, with efficacy).

But before all that, we must admit that the experience of recent successes (and failures) in literary and pictorial fame have taught us a great deal. (Mallarmé, Rimbaud.)

We have observed that daring in these fields *paid off*.

In short, here is the important point: TAKING THE SIDE OF THINGS *equals* TAKING ACCOUNT OF WORDS.

Certain texts will have more TST in the alloy, others more TAW . . . No matter. In either case, there must be the one *and* the other. Otherwise, nothing is gained.

(This is only one of the headings to be followed:)

"Start with words and go toward things." (Rolland de Renéville): not so.

We shall be reproached by some for expecting our ideas to come from words (dictionary, puns, rhymes, whatever . . .): indeed, we admit it. This has to be in the process, one has to respect raw material, foresee its

way of aging, etc. (cf. "Fragments Métatechniques"*).
However, we shall reply, this is not exclusive. We also
expect unbiased observation and a kind of cynicism, an
open-minded approach to uninhibited relationships, to
provide us with ideas.

Chosen form: definition-description esthetically and
rhetorically suitable.

Limit of the form: *its extent*. From the formula (or
concrete maxim) all the way to the novel, such as *Moby
Dick* for example.

Here we might explain that our age has lost the habit
of considering things from a somewhat eternal, serene,
sirian (from Sirius) viewpoint . . .

Sidi-Madani,
Monday, December 29
(late evening)

In the course of the essay, place ideas like these: after
"a certain feeling of queasiness as in the face of instability"—"non-resistance, defeat.")

Defeat or victory (in a theoretical discussion not followed by a vote, a precise result that alters the outside
world) is one and the same: as haphazard, ephemeral,
open to discussion, the one as the other.

And of course, this instability, this flaccid, disquieting
side to even the victorious ideas I come up with, is
something I myself suffer from: it is I who am defeated,
who hardly exist any more, who consider myself refuta-
ble, humiliated, even more than by a physical defeat.
My self-esteem suffers.

* *Nouveau Recueil*, Paris, Gallimard, 1967, pp. 15–17.

How then could I consent to spend my life in this condition: a spot criss-crossed by errors, blown by winds, a scaffolding that a flick of the finger can overturn? What is this stuffing, this mush I have in my mind? Even if it is victorious?

On the contrary, a splendid image, a daring, new and valid presentation: I am prouder of it than if I had evolved a system, invented a mechanism of prime importance, broken a record, discovered a continent. It is as though I had discovered a new metal; better yet, I discovered it *inside man,* and it is signed: it is I, it is the proof of my superiority over the whole world (from experience, I can be sure of the admiration of those who resemble me); I have given pleasure to the human mind.

Sidi-Madani,
Sunday, January 4, 1948 (1)

... Given pleasure to the human mind.

Not only given a chance to see, given pleasure in the sense of sight (the sight of the mind), no! Given pleasure to that sense at the back of the mouth, equidistant from mouth (tongue) and ears. Which is the sense of formulation, the Word.

What stems from there has more authority than anything else; the Law and the Prophets stem from there. The sense that takes even greater pleasure when one reads than when one listens (but also when one listens), when one recites (or declaims), when one-thinks-and-writes-it-down.

The kind of glance-that-is-spoken.

Sunday, January 4, 1948 (2)

At the outset some naïveté (or silliness) I suppose.

If *ideas* (do I mean by that just opinions? —perhaps) make me queasy, slightly nauseous (it's a fact), it must be because I am not very intelligent. Instinctively, I grant them an absolute value, where evidently they have only a *tactical* value. Thus they cannot fail to disappoint me. And the fact is they do disappoint me.

When I do happen to come out with some, since I do it with the same naïveté, forgetting their uniquely tactical value, and on the contrary, encouraged by heaven knows what momentary conviction (?), I immediately bite my nails. Of course! Whose fault? It was inevitable.

And so ideas are really not for me. He who handles them with ease can always get out of them: by rhetoric. Whereas it is they who handle me. I get furious. I feel duped. Then what shall I replace them with?

Well, the same naïveté makes me wish one agreed on facts, observations—or at least on definitions. Where what evidently happens is anything but agreement; merely discussion, and finally imposition—which is why, naturally, there is no need for definitions. Quite the contrary!

A degree of silliness and a lot of whorishness (coquettishness). I would like to please everybody.

As one can see, I have no doubts about myself!

So then, to work. Or, if you prefer, let's try to catch ourself at work, *in flagrante delicto* of creation. Here we
are in Algeria, trying . . .

Let's catch ourself in the act of creation.

Here we are in Algeria, trying to render the colors of
the Sahel (seen across the Mitidja, at the foot of the
Atlas). To a certain degree, the problem here is one of
expression.

After many falterings, we finally speak of a somewhat
sacripant pink. *A priori,* the word pleases us. Nevertheless, we consult the dictionary. It immediately refers us
from Sacripant to Rodomont (two characters in Ariosto).
Now then, Rodomont means Red Mountain, and he was
the king of Algeria. Q.E.D., *nothing more fitting.*

Lessons to be learned from this:

1. We can use *sacripant* as an adjective of color. It is
even recommended.

2. We can modify *rodomont* by using it in a softened
form: "The gentle rodomounting." In any case, we can
work around it.

Ideas are not my forte. I do not handle them with
ease. They handle me instead. Give me a queasy feeling,
nausea. I don't like to find myself thrown in their midst.
Objects in the external world, on the other hand, delight
me. They sometimes surprise me, but seem in no way
concerned about my approval: which they immediately
acquire. I do not question them.

I have published little more than a small book entitled *Le Parti Pris des Choses,* some five or six years
ago. And now that a few people have read it, a small
number among them have asked me for explanations of
it, desiring particularly that I reveal something about my
creative method, as they call it.

Naturally, I find that very kind. A bit embarrassing
also to be truthful, but I suppose I had to expect it.

Of course, to be completely sincere, I cannot conceive
of writing validly any other way but mine.

The first question I will ask is this: how does one
write?

Monday, January 5, 1948 (2)

Well, let me say it finally, for the reader will soon
realize that I begin by the end, so let me say it to begin
with: any old pebble, for example *this one* that I picked
up the other day on the bed of the Chiffa river, seems to
me capable of giving rise to fresh remarks of the *highest
interest.* And when I say *this one* and *highest interest,*
what I mean is this: this pebble, since I consider it a
unique object, arouses in me a particular feeling, or
perhaps it is rather a complex of particular feelings.
First I have to become aware of it. At this point, the
reader shrugs his shoulders and disclaims any interest
in such exercises. For, he says, there is nothing of man
in that. And what else could there be? Only it is man
until now unknown to man. A quality, a series of qualities, a composite of qualities, unwritten, unformulated.
That is why it is of highest interest. We are talking about
man of the future. Do you know anything more interesting? I am completely taken with it. Why am I so taken

with it? Because I think I can carry it off. On what condition? On condition of being single-minded, and obey-
ing *it*. Of not being satisfied with too little (or too
much). Of saying nothing that is not exclusively suited
to it. It is not so much a question of saying everything;
that would be impossible. Only what is suitable to it
alone, only what is valid. And to the limit: all that has
to be said is a simple valid thing. That is quite enough.

So here I am with my pebble, which intrigues me,
arouses in me untapped resources. With my pebble which
I respect. My pebble which I want to replace by an
adequate logical (verbal) formula.

Fortunately, 1) it persists; 2) my feeling at the sight
of it persists; 3) the dictionary is not far, I have the
feeling the right words are there. If not, then I will have
to create them. But words that can communicate, be con-
ductors of thought (as one says conductor of heat or
electricity). After all, I have the syllables, the onomatopeias, the letters. I'll get along just fine!

And I really think words will do . . .

This pebble won the victory (the victory of existence—
individual, concrete; the victory of coming into my
sight and coming to life with the word) because it is
more interesting than the sky. Not quite black, dark
gray rather, the size of half a rabbit liver (a rabbit has
nothing to do with this), nice in the hand. The right
hand, to be precise, with a hollow in which the outside
(when someone else looks at me) of my median finger's
last joint fits comfortably . . .

Sidi-Madani,
Friday, January 9, 1948

Nothing more ordinary than what is happening to me, nothing simpler than the solution to the problem before me.

My little book, *Le Parti Pris des Choses,* which appeared about six years ago, has given rise to a number of critical articles—generally rather favorable—which have spread my name in certain circles, even beyond the borders of France.

Although the very short texts which make up this slim collection contain no explicit thesis—philosophic, moral, esthetic, political, or other—most of the commentators have given them interpretations related to these diverse fields.

More recently, two or three critics have even begun to study the form of my texts.

The revue *Trivium* published one of these studies and, when I expressed my pleasure, asked me to supply a few comments of my own on what one of my more generous critics, Mrs. Betty Miller, called my creative method.

Sidi-Madani,
Saturday, January 10, 1948

"Turning to the poets," Socrates said, "I selected those of their poems that seemed to me most carefully constructed; I asked them what they had meant to say, for I wished to learn something from their company. Athenians, I am ashamed to tell you the truth; but I must nonetheless. Among all those present, almost everyone was able to give a better account of those poems than the ones who had written them. I quickly realized that it is not intellect which guides the poet, but natural inspiration, a fervor like that which transports sooth-sayers and fortune tellers; they all say very interesting things but understand nothing about what they are say-ing. This, in my estimation, is what poets experience also, and at the same time I came to realize that their talent for poetry led them to think they were equally gifted for everything else; which they were not. And so I left them too, convinced I was superior to them . . .

". . . Finally I turned to the artists. I was aware that I understood practically nothing about the arts, and knew I would make endless discoveries in their com-pany. In that I was not mistaken, for they knew many things that I did not, and in that respect were more capable than I. However, Athenians, the great artists struck me as having the same failing as the poets, for there was not one who, just because he excelled in his art, did not think himself highly versed in other fields of knowledge, even the most capital, and this failing undermined their capability. And so I questioned my-self . . . asking myself if I would prefer to be what I am without their capability and without their ignorance, or instead have their abilities and their failings. I re-plied . . . I would rather be what I am."

What emerges from the foregoing, if not (my apolo-gies) considerable silliness on Socrates' part? What an idea to ask a poet what he meant! And is it not obvious that if he is the only one unable to explain it, it is be-cause he can only say what he said the way he said it (otherwise he would probably have said it differently)?

From this I also gain the certainty of Socrates' inferi-ority to the poets and artists, not his superiority.

For if in fact Socrates is wise in that he recognizes

his ignorance and only knows that he knows nothing, and in fact Socrates knows nothing (except that), the poet and the artist on the other hand know at least what they have expressed in their carefully prepared works.

They know it better than those who can explain it (or think so), for they know it *in their own terms*. Furthermore, it is in these terms that everybody learns it and learns it easily by heart.

We shall soon be able to draw from all this a number of conclusions (or consecutive ideas). But first we must confess that poets and artists often abdicate their good fortune and wisdom, thinking they can explain their poems and believing that their ability in this technique enables them to resolve other kinds of problems, which is not necessarily so.

Let no one expect of me such presumption. Anybody is more capable than I of explaining my poems. Yet obviously I am the only one capable of producing them.

Could it be that the fact that a poem cannot be explained by its author is not to the shame of the poem and its author, but rather to his honor?

Surely, what would be entirely to my shame is if someone else said what I wanted to say better than I and convinced me of a fault (or a lack) for example, or of a redundancy, which I might have avoided. I for one would immediately correct such an error, for the poem's perfection is more important to me than any feeling of my own infallibility.

But then, could one say that a poem which can in no way be explained is by definition a perfect poem?

Certainly not. It must have still other qualities, and perhaps *one* only. Socrates may not have been as silly as he first seemed to us. And he may have had no idea whatever of asking for the explanation of a poem *that contained its own internal* e v i d e n c e . . . (But would it still be called a poem? . . .)

What does this evidence refer to? To a specific quality of expression (or means of expression)? In a sense, yes, but only in one sense. It refers equally to the pertinence, respect, adequacy (this is the most delicate), of that expression (in relation to itself absolutely perfect) for the perfection of the object (or an object) itself.

Here egoism and altruism become confused. One must be fierce and respectful at the same time. The way to do it is for the thing itself to be fierce . . . yet fall within human norms and categories. (It can do no less.)

—So? —So!
—Agreed? —Agreed!

1. Though of all my qualities I consider you the closest (the most specific well expressed . . .),
give in to the commonplace, you are made for it (. . . creates the commonplace).
2. Nothing is as interesting to express as that which is not easily conceived (the most specific).

Let that which is not easily conceived speak out clearly! (In the optative.)

At each moment during the labor of expression, step by step with the writing, language reacts, proposes its own solutions, incites, suscitates, assists in the formation of the poem.

No word is used which is not immediately considered an individual; whose inner light is utilized, and shadow too.

As soon as I allow a word to leave, as soon as I let it go, I immediately have to treat it not like any old thing, a stick of wood, a piece of a puzzle, but as a pawn or a figure, a person in three dimensions, etc. . . . and I can't do whatever I want with it. (Cf. Picasso's remark about my poetry.)

Each word imposes itself on me (and on the poem) in all its density, with all the associations it comprises (would comprise if it stood all alone, on a dark background). And yet, it has to be surmounted . . .

REGARDING TWO PERSONAL MECHANISMS

The first consists of placing the chosen object (explain how *duly* chosen) in the center of the world, that is, in the center of my "concerns"; opening a particular trap door in my mind, and thinking about it naïvely and fervently (lovingly).

Explain that it is not so much the object (it doesn't necessarily have to be present) as the idea of the object, including the word that designates it. The object as notion; the object in the French language, in the French mind (an actual listing in the French dictionary).

And then a certain cynicism creeps into the relationships. Cynicism is not the word (but had to be mentioned).

Everything that has ever been thought enters into it. Everything that will be thought, the measure of the object, its qualities, compared. Above all the most tenuous, the least often stated, the most shameful (though they appear to be arbitrary, puerile—or evoke a generally inadmissible order of relationships).

In other cases only *one* aspect of the object, my preferred reaction, my favorite association (peeling a boiled potato, and the way it cooks), will be emphasized, given prime importance.

One digs and one discovers. Here the trap door of sleep and dreams is as important as the one of lucidity and wakefulness.

Also important is not to let oneself be put off by habitually inadmissible associations of qualities. In fact, that is the heart of the matter: declaring the anomalies, proclaiming them, glorifying them, naming them—a new *character*.

For what matters is the character all this represents, seen from the good side, praised, applauded, approved, taken as a lesson, an example.

One point to be thoughtfully considered is this: I said just before that we were dealing with the object as idea, or notion, in which its name, the word habitually designating it, plays a very important part.

Quite so.

Thus at times the name helps me, when I happen to invent some justification for it, or seem to have discovered one in it (or so I convince myself).

But it also happens on occasion that this *partial* ensemble of characteristics, dealing more with the name of the object than with the object itself, gains on the others. This can be dangerous.

As to those characteristics of the object which depend less on its name than on something else, I must try to express them *despite the word* which might obscure them, annihilate them, replace them, pack them up (send them packing), after simplifying, bending and condensing them out of proportion.

Another way of approaching the thing is to consider it unnamed, unnameable, and describe it *ex nihilo,* but so well that it can be recognized—however, only at the end; its name, as it were, the last word of the text and not appearing until then.

Or appearing only in the title (given at the end).

The name must not be indispensable.
Replace the name.

Here, however, other dangers crop up. The concern to avoid mentioning the name can transform the poem into such a game, so artificial, so un-serious, that the result is like the periphrases of the abbé Delille.*

Whereas it has less to do with a comparative description *ex nihilo,* than with a word given to the object which should express its mute character, its lesson, in almost moral terms. (There has to be a bit of everything in it: definition, description, morality.)

A rhetorical form per object (that is, per poem)

If one cannot expect the object to take it upon itself to speak (prosopopoeia), which would be too easy a rhetorical form and would become monotonous, each object must nonetheless impose a particular rhetorical form on the poem. No more sonnets, odes or epigrams; the very form of the poem must in some way be determined by its subject.

Little in common between that and calligrams (Apollinaire); this has to do with a much more hidden form.

---

* Jacques Delille (1738–1813), French abbot and poet, translator of Virgil and Milton, famous for his ingenious periphrases.

. . . I do not say that I don't, on occasion, make use of certain devices of a typographical nature;

nor do I say that in each of my texts there is a relationship between its prosodic form (if I may call it that) and its subject;

but it does happen from time to time (and more and more frequently).

All that has to remain hidden, has to stay in the skeleton, never become apparent; sometimes it is only in the intention, the conception, the fetus: the way in which the word is caught, held, then let go.

No rules for that, precisely because they change (according to each subject).

Sidi-Madani,
Saturday, January 31, 1948

PLAN—Poems, not to be explained (Socrates). Superiority of poets over philosophers:

a) I am not really sure I am right in using the term "poet,"

b) superiority so long as they do not think themselves superior in anything but their poetry.

Poetic evidence. That, evidently, is open to question. There lies the danger. Poetic knowledge (poetry and truth).

From the specific to the general.

(Inclusion of humor: much wordplay.)

Two things bear the truth:

action (science, method) and poetry (damn the word); qualification?

—*the evidence of relationships of expression.*

If I define a butterfly as a *twice-spawned petal,* what could be *truer?*

Poems, not to be explained:

1. Poem-poems: because not logical. Objects.
2. Poem-formulas: more limpid, striking, decisive, than any explanation.

Superiority of poets over philosophers: they know what they are expressing in their own terms.

From the specific to the general:

the specific in the external world;

a rhetoric for each object;

it is always toward the proverbial that language tends.

Sidi-Madani,
Tuesday, February 3, 1948
during the night (1)

Nothing could be more flattering than what has happened to me, but it still makes me laugh when I think about it. This era must be weirdly impoverished for anybody to attach any importance to literature like mine! How can one be so mistaken?

All I ever did when writing the texts that make up *Taking the Side of Things* was to amuse myself, when the urge came over me, by writing only what could be written without wracking my brain, about the most ordinary things, selected completely by chance.

Really, it was an enterprise conceived of absolutely lightheartedly, without any intention of profundity and even, to be truthful, without the slightest seriousness.

I never said anything except what came into my head at the moment I said it on the subject of perfectly ordinary things, chosen entirely by chance.

Like those Barbary fig trees . . .

Sidi-Madani,
Tuesday, February 3, 1948
during the night (*2*)

I am not a great writer, you are mistaken gentlemen. Compared to La Fontaine (for example) I will never be more than a schoolboy. I construct with difficulty, build with much heaviness. Granted, I take a lot of trouble . . . (here my pen spat violently).
. . . This big blotch refutes me and forces me to give up this subject—and my humility!

Sidi-Madani,
Tuesday, February 3, 1948
(*morning*)

I am probably very lucky, for in fact I have not been asked to explain this or that piece but rather to reveal in some way the method by which they were produced. And perhaps this entitles me to assume that from the outset they are considered clear enough to be recognized, to be understood as *inexplicable,* so that I am merely asked to tell how I managed to produce texts that are so *inexplicable,* so obviously clear, so obvious.

As a matter of fact, this in itself is fairly amazing. For how is it possible to be so surprised by (or interested in) the obvious nature of a text that one thinks of asking how it was produced?

How to explain, except as inability or clumsiness natural to writing clearly, the desire to learn to write this way?

From the question asked of me, am I then to conclude

there is a degree of imbecility (or excessive complexity) in the minds of today?

Or can I perhaps infer something else (which would be more to my liking)?

Is it that some of my texts, for all their obviousness, have an unfamiliar, surprising quality—and that the surprise they cause (and the questions resulting from that surprise) stems less from their obviousness than from their strangeness? . . .

I would then have to conclude that there are two kinds of obviousness: the ordinary, which raises no questions; and the strange, which surprises and convinces at the same time.

Perhaps in this way I can get to the point surreptitiously . . .

Le Grau-du-Roi,
February 26, 1948

PROÊME—The day people are willing to accept as sincere and *true* the declaration I have repeatedly made that I do not consider myself a poet, that I *use* poetic magma *but only* to get rid of it, that I lean more toward conviction than superstition, that my concern is to arrive at *clear* and *impersonal* formulas,

they will make me happy,

they will save themselves a lot of pointless discussions about me, etc.

I aim toward definition-descriptions that take account of the current content of ideas—

for me and for the Frenchman of my time (*à la page* in the book of Culture, yet at the same time honest and genuine in his reading within himself).

My book has to replace 1) the encyclopedic dictionary, 2) the etymological dictionary, 3) the analogical dictionary (which does not exist), 4) the dictionary of rhymes (interior ones too), 5) the dictionary of synonyms, etc., 6) all lyric poetry inspired by nature, objects, etc.

Merely by wanting to account for the *total content of ideas about them,* I am drawn *by objects* away from traditional humanism, away from current man, and drawn ahead of him. I add to man the new qualities I name.

There you have *Taking the Side of Things.*

Taking Account of Words does the rest . . . Howevei, poetry as such does not interest me, in the sense that raw analogical magma is called poetry today. Analogies are interesting, but less so than differences. What is important is to grasp, through analogies, the differential quality. When I say that the inside of a walnut is similar to a praline, it is interesting. But even more interesting is their difference. To make one feel analogies, that is something. To name the differential quality of the walnut, that is purpose, that is progress.

Paris,
April 20, 1948

One must work starting from the *discovery* made by Rimbaud and Lautréamont (of the need for a new rhetoric*).

And not from the *question* raised by their early works.

Until now one has only worked starting from the question (or rather one has only restated the question more feebly).

* Rimbaud: "I now know how to greet beauty." Lautréamont: Poems (*passim*). [Author's note]

▣   The Silent World Is Our Only Homeland

Addressing the readers of a well-run newspaper, that is, one abounding in "capital" pronouncements of the "greatest" world-wide publicists, I need hardly inform them that we are doubtless running ahead on the prodromes of a new civilization, while for centuries the decay of the preceding one has been following along. Indications of the new era can be seen primarily in the painting of the Paris school since Cézanne, and in the French poetry of the 1870's. Only it seems that poetry has not quite caught up with painting in that it has produced fewer constructed works, works that make their impact by form alone (but we are seeing to that).

Since World War I everything has been dominated by the great schism in the declining civilization, which hastens evolution. Only the geniuses in painting, Braque in the lead, have been supporting the new spirit. And it is only as of the last few years (almost everyone having previously thought the contrary) that we can afford to congratulate ourselves for staying on *that side*, since the delightful anarchy prevailing there at least lets the seeds live, take root (more often than not in misery), survive in any event, and sometimes reach the surface.

In short, we know, only lately—and this is what is essentially MODERN—how civilizations are born, live and die. We know that after a period of discovering new values (always taken directly from the cosmos, but magnified and unrealistic), what follows is their elaboration, elucidation, dogmatization and refinement; we know above all, because in Europe we have been living with it since the Reformation, that as soon as values are dogmatized schisms arise, followed sooner or later by catastrophe.

Yes. That is what we cannot forget, and what many poets have understood. That, if it is anywhere, is the GREATNESS of modern man and, for the first time perhaps, PROGRESS (?). We know that we must necessarily go through the whole cycle I have just described, for such is the nature of man. At least we can try not to linger in either of these periods, and above all to get out of the dangerous classical period as fast as possible, that period of perfect mythology and dogmatization. So that, rather than end INEVITABLY in catastrophe, LET US IMMEDIATELY ABOLISH VALUES, in every work (and in every method), AT THE VERY MOMENT WE DISCOVER, ELABORATE, ELUCIDATE, REFINE THEM. This, in poetry for example, is the lesson learned from Mallarmé. This, moreover, is the point of all great masterworks and what makes them eternally valid; nothing can prevent the MEANINGS, which have been LOCKED into the humblest OBJECT or PERSON, from always *striking the hour*, the serial hour (of Hell or Paradise).

In these terms, one will surely understand what I consider to be the function of poetry. It is to nourish the spirit of man by giving him the cosmos to suckle. We have only to lower our standard of dominating nature and to raise our standard of participating in it in order to make the reconciliation take place. When man becomes proud to be not just the site where ideas and feelings are produced, but also the crossroad where they divide and mingle, he will be ready to be saved. Hope therefore lies in a poetry through which the world so invades the spirit of man that he becomes almost speechless, and later reinvents a language. Poets should in no way concern themselves with human relationships, but should get to the very bottom. Society, furthermore, takes good care of putting them there, and the love of things keeps them there; they are the ambassadors of the silent world. As such, they stammer, they murmur, they sink into the darkness of logos—until at last they reach the level of ROOTS, where things and formulas are one.

This is why, whatever one says, poetry is much more important than any other art, any other science. This is also why poetry has nothing in common with what appears in the poetry anthologies of today. True poetry is what does not pretend to be poetry. It is in the dogged drafts of a few maniacs seeking the new encounter.

It could well be that the very beauty of the world is what makes life so difficult for us. Did I say difficult? Beauty is the impossible which lasts. We have everything to say . . . and can say nothing; that is why we begin anew each day, on the widest variety of subjects and in the greatest number of imaginable procedures. We do not set out to write a BEAUTIFUL text, a beautiful page, a beautiful book. Absolutely not! We simply refuse to be DEFEATED: 1) by the beauty or fascination of Nature, or even the humblest object; nor do we recognize any hierarchy among the things to be said; 2) by language; we will continue to try; 3) we have lost all desire for relative success and all taste for admitting it. We couldn't care less about the usual criteria. Only lassitude stops us. The monopolization of these criteria by a few hucksters has thoroughly disinclined us from any further sermonizing on MEASURE or EXCESS. We know that we successively reinvent the WORST mistakes of every stylistic school of every period. So much the better! We don't want to say what we think, which is probably of no interest (as is evident here). We want to be UNSETTLED in our thinking. (Have I said it often enough? I'll say it again.)

The silent world is our only homeland. We make use of its possibilities according to the needs of the times.

1952

III

from Pieces*

* LE GRAND RECUEIL, vol. 3, Paris, Gallimard, 1961.

▣ The Shrimp in Every (and All in a) State

THE SHRIMP TEN TIMES SUMMONED (FOR ONE SUMMATION)

. . . Then from the depths of a watery chaos and a limpid density that can be distinguished from ink though poorly, I sometimes see rising up a tiny fearful question mark.

This little monster of circumspection, standing guard at the gates of his underwater dwelling, what does he want, where is he going?

Arched like a refined little finger, vial, translucent knick-knack, capricious vessel not unlike the capricorn beetle, vitreous chassis equipped with hypersensitive overanxious antennae, banquet hall, hall of mirrors, sanatorium, elevator—arched, cowering, glass-bellied, robed with a train ending in hairy paddles or coattails— he moves by jumps. Old chap, you have too many organs of circumspection. They will be your undoing.

I shall first compare you to a caterpillar, or a writhing gleaming worm, then to a fish.

Those stupid speeding bobbins, nibbling away with their noses in seaweed, will escape my sack more readily. Your organs of circumspection will detain you in my net, if I raise it fast enough out of the water— that environment unsuited to the unstoppered orifices of our senses, that natural washtub—unless by retrograde bounds (I was about to say retroactive, like a question mark), you return to the spacious recesses where the assumption—in unremembered depths, visionary heights— of the expert little diver takes place, as he spirals along, urged on by some vague impulse . . .

The shrimp, roughly the size of a knick-knack, has a consistency slightly softer than a fingernail, and practices the art of living in suspense within the worst marine confusion of the rocky hollows.

Like a knight on the road to Damascus suddenly struck by skepticism, it lives among its piled-up weapons, now wilted and transformed into organs of circumspection.

Its head under a helmet soldered to its thorax, generously fitted with antennae and feelers of extravagant delicacy . . . Endowed with the prompt power, residing in the tail, of a pack of unleashed hounds . . .

Standing guard at the gates of its underwater dwelling, almost motionless like a chandelier—by quick, jerky, successive, retrograde bounds, followed by quick returns, it escapes the direct onslaught of devouring maws, as well as any prolonged contemplation, any satisfactory ideated possession.

Nothing about it can be grasped at first, except that singular manner of fleeing which makes it seem to be some harmless optical illusion . . .

Assiduous, vulnerable . . .

First: circumstances. It lives in the worst marine confusion, in an environment inimical to our senses.

Second: quality. It is translucent.

Third: quality. It is encumbered by a profusion of hypersensitive organs of circumspection which cause it to jump backward on slightest contact.

Distinguished denizen of marine confusion, a transparency as useful as the way it jumps eliminates all continuity from its presence, even when immobile under scrutiny.

First: the shrimp's jump, cinematic theme. Stimula-
tion of the desire for clear perception, expressed by
millions of individuals.

Second: thanks to its not fleeing but haunting character, one slowly begins to grasp the following:

Third: a strange-looking knight whose wilted weapons
have become instruments of calculation and circumspection. Conquest through inquest.

Fourth: but there's the rub—too many organs of
circumspection lead it to its doom.

Revelation through death. A rosy death for the few
elect.

Each shrimp has a million chances of a gray death in
the mouth or gullet of some fish . . .

But a few elect, graced by the artificial elevation of
their environmental temperature, experience a revealing
death, a rosy death.

The shrimp's revealer is its cooking water.

Long ago perhaps, these animals, trusting their many
weapons, enjoyed noble confidence . . .

We do not know what great fright or deception made
them become so fearful.

Still, they have not yet taken to running away with
their back turned.

They back away, always facing forward.

Helmeted, bearing a lance, like a tiny Athena,
proud and pusillanimous, skittish but steadfast,
between two rocks, between two pools,
amid whirling waters,
it emerges fully armed;
it sets off in conquest, in inquest . . .

But it has too many organs of circumspection.
They will betray it.

Pursued by fate or hunted by his enemies, a god, once
among other gods, named Palaemon, entered the seas
and was adopted by them: evolved galley, animal its own
slave, gilled pentareme without a crew.

Standing guard at the gates of its underwater dwelling, silent shipwreck, almost dead, full-rigged at all
times, it feels out its freedom.

Then, amid the whirlings of icy waters in the hollows
of the rocks' gaping skulls, what vague impulse urges
it to expose itself, fearful little diver, summoned perhaps merely by a staring glance?

Body arched always ready to jump backward, it moves
forward slowly, constantly pursuing its meticulous inquest.

Its head in a helmet soldered to its thorax, to which its
abdomen is jointed, both compressed into a carapace,
but a vitreous flexible one,

Chewing legs, walking legs, swimming legs, feelers,
antennae, antennules: in all nineteen pairs of specialized
appendages,

Anachronistic vessel, you have too many organs of
circumspection; you will be betrayed by them.

Those stupid speeding bobbins, nibbling away with
their noses in seaweed, will escape my sack (of netting
to make you confuse it with liquid) more readily, leaving me with nothing but a cloud of mud.

Unless jump by jump—backward, jerky, unforeseeable—like the knight's jumps in the jungle of a three-
dimensional chessboard, you gain a temporary assumption into the spacious recesses of dreams, beneath the
rock from which I will not rise that easily discouraged.

The shrimp looks like certain harmless optical illusions in the form of dashes, commas, other equally simple signs—and jumps around not dissimilarly.

It is the quick-moving, fast-swimming species of the genus represented in the lower depths by the lobster, the prawn, the spiny lobster and, in cold streams, by the crayfish.

But is it any happier? That is another question . . .

It is considerably smaller than those heavy vehicles, its transparency is that of a fingernail, the consistency of its covering slightly softer.

Equipped with hypersensitive antennae, antennules, feelers, chewing legs, etc., all its power resides in its prompt tail which authorizes jumps that fool the eye, and save it from the direct onslaught of devouring maws.

All the squares of the three-dimensional chessboard are permissible, by virtue of its varied and unforeseeable jumps.

However, those jumps are restrained; its escape is not very far; its habits condemn it rigidly to this or that rock hollow.

Hardly more mobile than a chandelier, it is the distinguished denizen of marine confusion in the hollows of rocks.

In an upper circle of hell, it is a being condemned to a particular damnation. It ceaselessly feels out its freedom, it haunts emptiness.

Equipped with hypersensitive and cumbersome appendages, it is rigorously condemned to stay there because of its habits.

Impressively armed, even to the smallest details, its consistency remains nevertheless softer than a fingernail.

Its flight is short, its jumps restrained, and it returns ceaselessly to those places where its vulnerability is tested . . .

A circle of hell: the hollows of the rocks in the sea, with its various denizens, victims of particular damnations.

The condemnation of a being, in this environment of the worst marine confusion, in the hollows of rocks.

What vague impulse makes you leave these shores, carried off by the sea amid waves that ceaselessly and pitilessly contradict each other?

Equipped with antennules finer than Don Quixote's lance, dressed from head to tail in a cuirass, but of the transparency and consistency of a fingernail, its fleshly cargo seems to be nil . . .

Numerous qualities or circumstances make the shrimp the shyest object in the world, one which most successfully defies contemplation.

First of all, it appears most frequently in places where confusion is always at its peak: in the hollows of underwater rocks where liquid undulations ceaselessly contradict each other, where the eye in a limpid density barely distinguishable from ink never sees anything with certainty despite all its efforts.

In addition, endowed with hypersensitive antennae, it retracts on contact. Its jumps are very quick, jerky, retrograde, and are followed by slow returns.

That is why this superior arthropod is related to the kind of harmless optical illusions that are caused in man by fever, hunger, or simply fatigue.

Finally, and as effectively as those jumps which withdraw it to the least foreseeable squares of the three-dimensional chessboard, a useful transparency eliminates any manner of continuity, even when its presence is immobile under scrutiny.

. . . It blushes when dying in a certain way, through
the elevation of its environmental temperature . . .

Nothing more expert, nothing more discreet.

A hunted god entered the seas.
A sunken galley evolved.

From the meeting of these two disasters
A beast was born, forever circumspect;

The shrimp is that monster
of circumspection.

THE SHRIMP EXAGGERATED

One can imagine no place unknown to you, flat on your
belly, with your transparent insect-like roof, obtected by
all the details of the universe, your vitreous chassis with
its hypersensitive antennae that goes anywhere, defer-
ential to everything, wise, exacting, fearful, orthodox,
inflexible.
  Shrimp of the azure depths and craggy holes, monster
of the prompt tail that fools the eye; skeptical, arched,
doubtful, fictive, shrinking shrimp, universally docu-
mented by an ever-searching periscope, but retracting
on contact; fugacious, unobtrusive, stupefying nothing,
no thrashing coelenterate tentacles, no plumes, floating
at will.
  Monster on the alert, on the alert for everything, on
the alert for the discovery of the smallest parcel of sea
floor, the smallest territory yet unknown to the common-
est of strollers; watchful and calm, secure in the value,

speed and accuracy of its instruments of inspection and calculation: nothing more knowledgeable, more discreet.

Mysterious chassis, framework of many things, stable, immobile, relaxed, indifferent to the cold movement of eye and touch, carrying around something like the narrow beam of a lighthouse in daylight, yet its passing is noticed, noted at fixed dates in the most deserted places—the beaches, the high seas of the earth, the inner theater of the rocks.

—All the way to places where solitude, seen three-quarters from behind, walks on unaware of the glance that drinks it in, like a praying mantis, or any other phantom with a small head attached to a wandering body —aimless, but with seriousness and a certain fatality in its walk, wrapped in veils to keep its form imprecise.

Majestically, feeling the narrow beam of the light-house on the expanse, but without delay, impassive, un-grimacing, causing an indraft of nobility and grandeur, a sort of shadow or statue preceding me by only a few yards:

It could be a human being, a figure out of an allegory, or a grasshopper, though it does not advance by leaps and bounds, but by a steady walk, alternately placing its feet on the ground; the face, of which one only sees a vague profile, could be blind; its veils cloak it in such a way that the volume of its members seems greatly increased, the whole thing producing a constant waving or gesture intended to be followed by another.

Not only across swirling sands, but keeping fast be-hind, following with eye and step, with a feeling of re-spectful joy, without obligation, or sadness, assured of its mute protection,

its veils making it possible to follow it, to keep it

in sight without having to overlook the landscape—all the while maintaining its lead, its poise, never turning its head—a man, a child wandering along, unperturbed by the route he is forced to follow, nor by the pace maintained, nor even by the length of the walk,

who suddenly—on sitting down at the edge of the dune, which occurs as soon as fatigue has advised him to rest and give in to what is called taking stock of oneself—feels all sorts of gusts and puffs of delicious temperature on him, around him, holding on to his face, his ankles, his wrists and cheeks, during the assumption of the crayfish in azure depths.

ABODE OF THE GRAY SHRIMP

There, the wave, which returns to meet itself and is instantly rebuked and spat upon by its own family, retracts and admits its error. It falls into despair, displays its dishevelment, its self-made resolderings, etc.

(Absurd confusion of gravity.)

It is there, in the midst of constant remorse, constant upheaval of remorse (the opposite of bourgeois domestic life), of permanent repentance, it is there, where the swell persists, where cold broths are in commotion (whereas a perfectly reassured and reassuring pebble sinks to the bottom), that the shrimp is rigorously condemned by its habits.

It is there

In the churning waves

In the chilly broths

(also a consequence of the differences in temperature that start up, stir around, send off winds, and later, waves),

In the absurd confusion of gravity, playing against, struggling against other forces . . .

(the game: the clock game, to be precise; that is, an equilibrium slow to establish itself, which passes itself, repasses itself, etc. . . . .)

That is where, that is precisely where the shrimp, in order to live . . .

(The fact that life is a chemical phenomenon also explains the confusion that characterizes it, the incessant struggle of conflicting forces. These things go together. Along with repentance. And regret.)

. . . is rigorously condemned by its habits.

It seems clear that the shrimp is aware of the confusion, the incessant contradictions of the environment in which it lives, while for fish it is dull tranquility: in no way are they bothered by these contradictory influences, nor does it seem they have to be aware of them.

If they are bothered by anything, it seems rather to be by the consistency of the environment, the heaviness of the air they breathe. One sees their mouths gaping, their eyes goggling. They seem to be living on the constant brink of asphyxia and resurrection.

Respiration for them is a complicated process. They have to dissociate the air in water. Most of their time is probably taken up with that, is spent on that. (At this point I am reminded of myself, spending most of my time trying to breathe economically: earning money. It takes nine hours a day . . . While for others, breathing comes so easily: for that, they have money in their pockets, that oxygen . . . But we, we have to work hard to extract money from work, from time, from fatigue.)

. . . But for the shrimp it isn't that at all. No. If it has a problem, it is not breathing, but stabilizing itself in

the contrary currents that knock it against the rocks . . .
And also fleeing, because of the cumbersome nature of
its superfluous organs of circumspection.

(A problem that also reminds me of myself: we know
others like that, in an era bereft of faith, rhetoric, unity
of political action, etc. . . ., etc. . . .)

And so, while other forms—girdled, outlined by a
simple, solid form—merely pass through these underwater lanes (these halls, rooms, alcoves) brightly,
darkly, or sequined, in any event, opaque fugitives who
will not return—following mysterious migrations as pre-
determined as the movement of the stars—the shrimp,
almost immobile like a chandelier, haunts them, seems
rigorously condemned to them by its habits. Its daring
constantly brings it back to the very place its terror made
it vacate.

With each rock hollow the shrimp forms a permanent
esthetic unity (not only esthetic), thanks to its particular
density and the transparency of its flesh; to the complexi-
ties of its contours which take hold there and become in-
tegrated like the teeth of gears; thanks also to the restrained jumps which keep it there (even better perhaps
than immobility).

Like the first crystal formed from a liquid, like the
first constellation born of a nebula, the shrimp is the
pure Guest, the ideal Guest, the elect Guest, perfectly
suited to this environment.

For it never stops exploring it, prospecting it, sound-
ing it, examining it, feeling it, conducting a meticulous,
fastidious inquiry about it, fearing it (fearing everything in it), feeling pain and anguish on its account,
discovering it, haunting it; in short, making it habitable.

If on occasion it forgets the bonds of its nature and tries to rush off like a fish, it soon sees its error: there, and in that way, is the shrimp condemned to live . . .

It is the chandelier of confusion.
It is a monster of circumspection.
(Likewise, in troubled times, the poet.)

It must also be noted that the shrimp is the fleeting shadow, the form capable of fleeting—small, tenuous, good swimmer—among a genus represented in the depths by the spiny lobster, the prawn, the lobster, and in icy streams by the crayfish: all of them much heavier, bigger, stronger, better armed, more down to earth. The shrimp is like the translucent shadow, scaled down but miraculously just as concrete, of those enormous beings, those ponderous vehicles. But does that mean its fate is any happier?

Long ago, perhaps because of all its weapons, it may have enjoyed noble perfection and self-assurance, but after some unknown deception or great fright, it became extremely timorous . . .

The shrimp's jump: a sideways leap, unexpected, like the knight in the chessboard jungle; a leap that allows it to parry the attack of devouring maws. Jerky, oblique jumps.

Breaking away on contact, without however dashing out of sight (it is rather when the shrimp does not move that one loses sight of it), revealing itself thereafter in such a way as to raise doubts, not about its identity, but about the possibility of a study or somewhat prolonged contemplation of it, which might ultimately lead to some kind of esthetic grasp . . . Consequent arousal of the desire or need for clear perception . . . Shyness of the object as object.

Finally, however well-armed, however endowed with perfection, it still needs a revelation to become entirely confirmed in its own identity; and that revelation is known to few individuals among the species: through a privileged death, a rosy death, when their natural environment is raised to a high temperature.

The shrimp's revealer is its cooking water.

SHRIMP ONE

The worst marine confusion in the hollow of rocks contains a being the length of a little finger, about as hard as a fingernail, about whom nothing can be grasped at first except its singular manner of running away.

Endowed with the prompt power, residing in its tail, of a pack of hounds suddenly released—by means of rapid, unexpected, jerky, retrograde jumps, followed by slow returns, it escapes the direct onslaught of devouring maws as well as any examination.

A transparency as useful as the way it jumps further eliminates continuity from even its stationary presence under scrutiny.

But fate, or compulsion, or daring, incessantly leads it back to the place from which its fright made it withdraw to begin with. Whereas other denizens, solidly and simply built, merely pass through these submarine grottoes as shadows or sparkles—as opaque runaways, in any case, not returning—the shrimp, virtually motionless, like a chandelier, seems rigorously condemned there by its habits.

It lies in the midst of its heaped-up weapons, its head under a helmet soldered to its thorax, generously equipped with antennae and feelers of extravagant sensitivity.

Oh, translucent vessel, indifferent to lures, you have too many organs of circumspection: you will be betrayed by them.

Those stupid speeding bobbins that nibble away with their noses in seaweed will escape from my sack more readily, leaving me with nothing but a cloud of mud—while you only achieve a temporary assumption in the spacious recesses under the rock from which I will not rise so easily discouraged.

Shrimp Two

Several characteristics or circumstances make a tiny animal one of the shyest things in the world and probably the most elusive object there is for contemplation; an animal it is less important to name right off than to evoke with prudence, allow to enter of its own accord (via pits and passages) into the conduits of circumlocution, and ultimately, to capture by words at the dialectic meeting point of its form, its environment, its mute condition, and the practice of its due profession.

Let us begin by admitting that there are times when a man's vision, upset by fever, hunger or simply fatigue, undergoes a temporary and probably harmless hallucination: from one end of his scope to the other, he sees a host of little signs moving in a particular way—in rapid, irregular, successive, backward jumps, followed by slow returns—indistinct, translucent, shaped like dashes, commas or other punctuation marks which, without hiding the world from him in any way, somehow obliterate it, move from place to place by superimposition, and finally make him want to rub his eyes so that by getting rid of them he can see better.

Now then, in the realm of external spectacles, an

analogous phenomenon sometimes occurs: the shrimp, deep within the waves it inhabits, jumps around in a not dissimilar fashion, and just as the spots I mentioned above were the result of an optical disturbance, so this little creature seems at first to be the outgrowth of marine confusion. The shrimp is most often seen in places where even in calm weather this confusion is always at its peak: in the hollows of rocks where liquid ripples constantly contradict each other, in this pure density barely distinguishable from ink, where the eye never sees anything for sure despite all its efforts. A transparency as useful as the way it jumps eliminates all continuity from its presence, even when immobile under scrutiny.

At this very point it becomes imperative that blurred illusion, encouraged by doubt and difficulty, not prevail over reason; illusion by which the shrimp—because our thwarted scrutiny passes almost at once into memory—would be remembered as no more than a reflection, or the fleeting fast-swimming shadow of species represented more tangibly on the sea bottom by lobsters or prawns, and in icy streams by crayfish. No, without a doubt, the shrimp is just as alive as those clumsy vehicles and knows, though its condition is less down-to-earth, all the pain and suffering that life anywhere entails . . . If the extreme inner complexity that at times animates them is not to prevent us from honoring the more characteristic forms of a stylization to which they are entitled—treating them later, when necessary, as mere ideograms—then we must not allow this use to spare us the sympathetic suffering which the observation of life irresistibly arouses in us—the price, no doubt, of an accurate understanding of the animate world.

What can add greater interest to a form than the observation that its reproduction and dissemination

throughout nature occurs in millions of copies at the
same time everywhere, in fresh and salt water, in good
weather and bad? Though many individuals suffer from
this form and its particular damnation, wherever this
phenomenon occurs we feel arise in us a desire for clear
perception. Objects that as objects are shy, appear to
raise less doubt about the reality of each individual than
about the possibility of a somewhat prolonged contemplation of it, a somewhat satisfying ideated possession;
prompt power, residing in the tail, of a pack of hounds
suddenly tearing loose: it is probably in the cinema
rather than in architecture that a theme like this can
finally be used . . . First the art of living had to be seen
to: we should have taken up that challenge.

1926–1934

◻ **The Pigeon**

Grain-fed belly, come down over here,
Saintly gray pigeon belly . . .

The way a storm rains, walks on broad talons,
Floats over, takes over the lawn,
Where first you rebounded
With the charming cooings of the thunder.

Show us soon your rainbow throat . . .

Then fly away obliquely, in a great flapping of wings
that pull, pleat, or rent the silken cover of the clouds.

1925

◨ The Frog

When little matchsticks of rain bounce off drenched fields, an amphibian dwarf, a maimed Ophelia, barely the size of a fist, sometimes hops under the poet's feet and flings herself into the next pond.

Let the nervous little thing run away. She has lovely legs. Her whole body is sheathed in waterproof skin. Hardly meat, her long muscles have an elegance neither fish nor fowl. But to escape one's fingers, the virtue of fluidity joins forces with her struggle for life. Goitrous, she starts panting . . . And that pounding heart, those wrinkled eyelids, that drooping mouth, move me to let her go.

1937

◨ The Horse

Many times the size of man, the horse has flaring nostrils, round eyes under half-closed lids, cocked ears and long muscular neck.

The tallest of man's domestic animals, and truly his designated mount.

Man, somewhat lost on an elephant, is at his best on a horse, truly a throne to his measure.

We will not do away with the horse, I hope?

He will not become a curiosity in a zoo?

. . . Already now, in town, he is no more than a miserable substitute for the automobile, the most miserable means of traction.

Ah, the horse is also—does man suspect it?—something else besides! He is *impatience* nostrilized.

His weapons are running, biting, bucking.

He seems to have a keen nose, keen ears, and very sensitive eyes.

The greatest tribute one can pay him is having to fit him with blinders.

But no weapon . . .

Whereby the temptation to add one. One only. A horn.

Thereby the unicorn.

The horse, terribly nervous, is aerophagous.

Hypersensitive, he clamps his jaws, holds his breath, then releases it, making the walls of his nasal cavities vibrate loudly.

That is why this noble beast, who feeds on air and grass alone, produces only straw turds and thunderous fragrant farts.

Fragrant thunderisms.

What am I saying, feeds on air? Gets drunk on it. Sniffs it, savors it, snorts it.

He rushes into it, shakes his mane in it, kicks up his hind legs in it.

He would evidently like to fly up in it.

The flight of clouds inspires him, urges him to imitation.

He does imitate it: he tosses, prances . . .

And when the whip's lightning claps, the clouds gallop faster and rain tramples the earth . . .

Out of your stall, high-spirited over-sensitive armoire, all polished and smoothed!

Great beautiful period piece!

Polished ebony or mahogany.

Stroke the withers of this armoire and immediately it has a faraway look.

Dust cloth at the lips, feather mop at the rump, key in the lock of the nostrils.

His skin quivers, irritably tolerating flies, his shoe hammers the ground.

He lowers his head, leans his muzzle toward the ground and consoles himself with grass.

A stepstool is needed to look on the upper shelf.

Ticklish skin, as I was saying . . . but his natural impatience is so profound, that inside his body the parts of his skeleton behave like pebbles in a torrent!

Seen from the apse, the highest animal nave in the stable . . .

Great saint! Great horse! Beautiful behind in the stable . . .

What is this splendid courtesan's behind that greets me, set on slim legs, high heels?

Giant goose of the golden eggs, strangely clipped.

Ah, it is the smell of gold that assails my nostrils!

Leather and manure mixed together.

Strong-smelling omelette, from the goose of the golden eggs.

Straw omelette, earth omelette, flavored with the rum of your urine, dropping from the crack under your tail . . .

As though fresh from the oven, on a pastry sheet, the stable's rolls and rum balls.

Great saint, with your Byzantine eyes, woeful, under the harness . . .

A sort of saint, humble monk at prayer, in the twilight.

A monk? What am I saying? . . . A pontiff, on his
excremental palanquin! A pope—exhibiting to all com-
ers a splendid courtesan's behind, generously heart-
shaped, on slender legs ending elegantly in high-heeled
shoes.

WHAT IS THIS CLACKING OF THE BIT?

THESE DULL THUDS IN THE STALL?

WHAT'S GOING ON?

PONTIFF AT PRAYER?

SCHOOLBOY IN DETENTION?

GREAT SAINTS! GREAT HORSES (HORSES OR HEROES?),
OF THE BEAUTIFUL BEHIND IN THE STABLE,

WHY, SAINTLY MONK, ARE YOU WEARING RIDING
BREECHES?

—INTERRUPTED DURING HIS MASS, HE TURNED HIS
BYZANTINE EYES TOWARD US . . .

                                    1948–1951

□ **Manure**

Straw rolls, easily crumbled. Steamy, smelly. Smashed
by wagon wheels, or spared by the breadth of the axle.

You have come to be thought of as something precious.
Still, you are scooped up with a shovel. This shows
human respect. It is true your odor would cling to the
hands.

In any case, you are not beyond the pale, nor as
repulsive as the droppings of dogs and cats, which have
the misfortune of too closely resembling man's in their
mortar-like pastiness and annoying stickiness.

                                    1932

◨ The Goat

> And if hell is myth in the heart of
> the earth, it is true in my heart.
>   MALHERBE

To Odette

Our tenderness at the notion of the goat is immediately
aroused because, between her frail legs, she carries
around all that milk—swelling the bagpipe with its down-
cast thumbs which the poor thing badly hides under the
rug passing for a shawl that always lies askew on her
rump—obtained through the nibbled means of a few
sparse herbs, or vines, of aromatic essence.

"Mere nibblings, you said it," they'll tell us. True,
but tenacious all the same.

And that bell which never stops.

All that fuss, she chooses to think, for the grace of
her offspring, that is, for raising this little wooden stool
that jumps around in place on four legs doing jetés
until, following his mother's example, he behaves more
like a stepstool, placing his forelegs on the first natural
step he can find, so as to graze even higher than what
lies within easy reach.

And capricious to boot, headstrong!

However small his horns, he affronts anything.

"Ah! Those kids are getting our goat," they mutter—
untiring wet-nurses and remote princesses, like the galaxies—and kneel down to rest. Head high, moreover,
and under heavy lids a fabulous starry-eyed look. However, uncrucifying their stiff limbs with a sudden effort,
they get up almost at once, for they do not forget their
duty.

These long-eyed beauties, hairy as beasts, beauteous and at the same time bumptious—or better said, Beelzebumptious—when they bleat, what are they bewailing? what torment? what distress?

Like old bachelors, they are fond of newspapers and tobacco.

And in connection with goats, one should doubtless mention rope, and even (what pullings! what placid jerking obstinacy!) rope at the end of its rope, a rope whip.

That goatee, that grave accent . . .

They haunt rocky places.

With a perfectly natural inflection, psalmodizing a bit from here on—we too going a bit far to seize the verbal occasion by the horns—let us, head high, make it known that *chèvre* (goat), not far from *cheval* (horse), but feminine with a grave accent, is merely a modulated modification which prances neither up nor down but rather climbs, with its last syllable, up those jagged rocks, up to the take-off area, the aerie of the mewt *e*.

No galloping with that in sight, however. No triumphal leap. None of those bounds, halted at the edge of the precipice by the shudder of failure along the chamois' skin.

No. For having reached those heights step by step, brought closer and closer by her researches—and missing the point—it would seem she apologizes humbly, lips atremble.

"This is really not for me," she stammers. "I'll not be caught here again." —and clambers down to the first bush.

This, in fact, is how the goat most often appears to us in the mountains, or in those regions cast off by nature: clinging, ragged animal, to bushes, ragged plants, themselves clinging to ragged minerals—those jagged cliffs, crumbled stones.

And she doubtless seems so pitiful for being, from a certain viewpoint, no more than that: a faulty tatter, a tether, a miserable accident; a hopeless approximation; a somewhat sordid adaptation to contingencies themselves sordid; and in the end, nothing but shreds.

And yet, here is a machine—a model germane to ours and thus fraternally cherished by us; by that I mean, within the realm of vagrant animation long ago conceived and perfected by nature—for obtaining milk under the hardest conditions.

It may be no more than a pathetic and pitiable animal, yet still a prodigious organism, a being, and it works.

So that the goat, like all creatures, is both an error and the accomplished perfection of that error; and thus deplorable and admirable, fearful and fascinating at once.

And we? Surely we can find enough satisfaction in trying to express this (imperfectly).

Thus shall I, each day, have loosed the goat on my note pad: sketch, draft, scrap of a study, as the goat herself is loosed on the mountain by her owner, against those bushes, those rocks—those hazardous thickets, those inert words—from which she is barely distinguishable at first glance.

And yet, on observing carefully, *she* lives, *she* moves. If one approaches, she pulls on her rope and tries to flee. One need not press her too hard to draw from her at once some of that milk, more precious and fragrant than any other—smelling like the spark of flint, furtively suggesting the metallurgy of hell—but exactly like the milk of the stars splattered across the night sky by reason of such violence, and whose infinite multitude and distance makes of their light this milt—drink and seed in one—diffused ineffably within us.

Nourishing, soothing, still warm, ah, surely it befits us to drink this milk, but in no way take pride in it. Any more, finally, than in the sap of our words, so long destined for us, perhaps—by way of the kid and the goat—as merely some obscure regeneration.

Such at least is the meditation of the grown-up buck.

Magnificent knucklehead, this dreamer, grandly flouting his ideas, bears their weight but not without some testiness useful for the brief acts assigned him.

These thoughts, formulated as weapons on his head, for motives of high civility curve backward ornamentally;

Knowing full well, moreover—though of occult source and readily convulsive in his deep sacks—

With what, with what love, he is burdened.

Here then, his phraseology on his head, is what he ruminates between two sallies.

1953–1957

□　Metamorphosis

At the foot of the stems twist as you will
The elastic of your heartstrings

It is not as a caterpillar
That you will get to know the flowers

When many a sign heralds
Your flight toward happiness

. . . .

He quivers and in a single leap
Joins the butterflies.

1944

◘ Clearing in Winter

Blue breaks through the gray, like the pulp from a black grape.

The whole atmosphere is like a brimming eye from which the need and desire to pour down have momentarily vanished.

But the downpour has left souvenirs everywhere that serve as mirrors for the clearing.

There is something touching about the relationship between two different moods. Something disarming about this halted effusion.

Each puddle then becomes a butterfly wing under glass,

But a passing wheel can make the mud fly up.

1932

▣ Landscape

The horizon, overscored with misty accent marks, seems
to be printed in small letters, of darker or lighter ink
depending on the light.
What lies closer gives me no more pleasure than a
painting,
What lies still closer, no more than sculpture or
architecture,
As to the reality of things right up to my knees, like
food, a feeling of real indigestion.
Until finally, everything sinks into my body and flies
out through my head, as though through a chimney open
to the sky.

1933

▣ Pastoral Symphony

Two-thirds up from the left shutter, a nest of bird songs,
a ball of bird calls, a skein of chirpings, a gurgling bird-
callogenous gland,
While a lamellibranch obstructs it crosswise,
(Everything wrapped in the fatty fluff of cloud-filled
sky)
And the burping of toads makes visceral noises
The cuckoo beats steadily like a distant heart throb.

1937

◙   The Water of Tears

To cry or see one cry is rather embarrassing to see:
between crying and seeing too many charms are inter-
spersed . . . But between seeing and crying are so many
connections that between crying and seeing we cannot
watch the tears.
(*He takes the woman's head in his hands.*)
Dearest head! What's going on in there?
Clinging to the cranial rock, the nicest little octopus
ever would remain there quietly—serving, for each bat-
ting of the lashes, merely as a burette—if some sudden
surge of sentimental tide, some violent seizure (regret-
table or welcome) did not at times press it (harder) to
express itself (better).
(*He leans over.*)
Dearest face! And what happens then?
A little globule pearls in the corner of the eye. Tepid,
salty . . . Clear, convincing . . .
(*She smiles.*)
This is how at times a face glows!
This is how at times one can gather from man's head
something that reaches him from the deepest realities—
the marine world . . .
The brain, by the way, smells of fish! Contains a
good bit of phosphorus . . .
(*She starts to cry again.*)
Ah, if between seeing and knowing there is some
connection, then from knowing to crying there must be
still others!
To cry or see one cry is rather embarrassing to see . . .
But I do think about it . . .
(*He collects a tear from the edge of his lashes.*)

From the eye to the slide of a microscope, is it not, conversely, a teardrop that is appropriate?

"Oh, pearls of Amphitrite! SUCCESSFUL EXPRESSIONS!

"Between the water of tears and the water of the sea there can only be a slight difference, if—in that difference, all of man perhaps . . ."

Laboratory comrades, please verify.

1944

◻ The Word Smothered by Roses

There's something excessive about a rose, like many plates piled up in front of a dinner guest.

There's something excessive about naming a girl Rose, for it assumes she must always be naked or gowned for a ball, when, perfumed by many dances, radiant, excited, she blushes moistly, pearling, cheeks aflame under the crystal chandeliers; tinted like a toast forever burnished by the oven.

The rose's green leaves, green stem with caramel highlights, and thorns—anything but caramel!—are of great importance to its nature.

There is a way of forcing roses which is reminiscent of what one does to fighting cocks when, to hasten the process, one puts steel spurs on them.

Oh, the fascination of helicoidogabalesque petulvas! The peacock's fan is a flower too, vulva-calyx . . . Prurience or itch: tickling produces budding, swelling, gaping. They puff up their gowns, their petticoats, their panties . . .

Flesh mixed with gowns, like kneaded satin: that is the substance of flowers. Each one gown and thigh together (breast and bodice too) which can be held with two fingers—at last! and handled as such; can be brought close to or moved away from one's nostrils; can be left, forgotten, taken back; arranged, opened up, looked into—and withered, as needed, by a single terrible bruise, from which there is no recovery: of bitter usefulness, causing, as it were, a return to the leaf stage —which love, for a young girl, takes at least a few months to accomplish . . .

Finally in bloom! Abated, their crises of aggressive neurasthenia!

That battling bush, perched on its spurs and fluffing its feather, will soon lose a bloom or two . . .
Graded shadings of superimposed saucers.
Tender shield rising up around a tiny mound of fine dust, more precious than gold.

In short, roses are like baked goods. The heat above inhales them, inhales what moves toward it (soufflés, for example) . . . tries to press against it, but can only go so far and no further; which then parts its lips, sends up its gassy parts, and burns . . . This is how baked goods redden, blacken, then smoke and burn: what happens is like a flowering in the oven, and the Word is merely . . .

Here is another reason for watering plants; for the humid principles, corrupted by heat, are what lead all other plant principles to their elevation.

The same impetus makes the blooms unstopper their bottles—permanently. They will use any means for showing off. Afflicted with a distressing infirmity (paralysis of their lower limbs), they wave their (perfumed) hankies . . .

For in their view—and not only roses, any flower—the rest of the world is always about to depart.

1949–1950

◘ The Plate

Consecrating it though we are, let us refrain from over-nacre-ing this everyday object. No prosodic ellipses, however brilliant, to say, flatly enough, a humble inter-position between pure spirit and appetite.

Not without humor, alas (the animal much better behaved!), was the name of its lovely surface taken from a shellfish. We, vagrant species, may not sit on it. It was named porcelain from the Latin—by analogy—*porce-lana*, sows's vulva . . . How's that for the appetite?

But all beauty which—of necessity, born of the in-stability of the waves—plates a conch shell . . . How's that for the pure spirit?

Whatever the case may be, the plate was born in this way of the sea: immediately multiplied, what's more, by that benevolent juggler who on occasion stealthily replaces the somber old man who grudgingly throws us one sun per day.

This is why you see the plate here in a number of species still vibrating, like ricochets caught on the sacred cloth of linen.

That's all there is to say about an object which offers more to live with than to contemplate.

1951

▣ Olives

Olive green, drab, black.

Olive drab somewhere between green and black, on the road to carbonization. A gentle carbonization, in oil—mixed in, perhaps, with the thought of rancidness.

But . . . is that right?

Does each olive, from green to black, pass through olive drab? Or is it not, in some cases, a sickness instead?

It would seem to come from the pit, which tries, pretty basely in that case, to exchange some of its hardness for the tenderness of the pulp . . . Instead of sticking to its business which, on the contrary, is not to harden the pulp but to harden itself against the pulp . . . So as to dishearten it to the point where it decomposes . . . enabling it, the pit, to reach the ground—and bury itself. Free from then on (but only then) to relax: to open up . . . and germinate.

Whatever the case, the circumflex on *olivâtre** is read with pleasure. It stands there like a heavy black eyebrow under which something swells up at once, while decomposition is getting ready.

When an olive turns black, nothing is more brilliantly so. What a marvel, that shriveled side within the form! . . . Tasty to the utmost, and shiny but not too, with nothing taut about it.

An even better oral suppository than prunes.

* Olive-colored.

Having rambled on enough about the color of the pulp and its form, let's get to the heart of the matter—which matters if one sucks the pit—that is, the closeness between *olive* and *ovale*.

Now here is a closeness well played, and how naïve. What could be more naïve, in fact, than an olive.

Graceful and deft in society, they are not for all that cloying, like some others: Jordan almonds . . . pretentious things!

More on the bitter side, in fact. And perhaps to be sweetened, they have to be treated in a certain way: left to marinate a bit.

Moreover, what one ultimately finds on reaching the pit is not an almond, but a little ball; a tiny torpedo of very hard wood, which could, given the chance, easily penetrate the heart . . .

Now, now! Let's not exaggerate! Let's smile instead (at least on one side of the mouth), so as to place it before long on the edge of the plate . . .

What could be simpler. In taste neither too good nor too bad . . . Requiring no more perfection than I have put into it . . . yet capable of pleasing, generally pleasing to most people, as an appetizer.

1947

◻ The Potato

To peel a boiled potato of good quality is a choice pleasure.

Between the pad of the thumb and the point of the knife held in the fingers of the same hand, one grasps

—after incising it—that rough thin paper by one of its lips, and pulls it toward one to detach it from the appetizing flesh of the tuber.

This easy operation, when performed without too many tries, leaves one with a feeling of inexpressible satisfaction.

The slight rustle made by the detaching tissues is sweet to the ear, and the discovery of the edible pulp delightful.

One feels—on observing the perfection of the bared fruit, the difference, the similarity, the surprise, and the ease of the operation—that one has accomplished something right and proper, long foreseen and desired by nature, but which one has the merit of fulfilling nonetheless.

This is why I shall say no more about it, running the risk otherwise of appearing complacent over too simple a task. I merely needed—in a few effortless phrases— to bare my subject by going precisely around its form; leaving it intact but clean, shining, and ready to experience as to provide the pleasure of its consumation.

. . . This taming of the potato by submitting it to boiling water for twenty minutes is quite amazing (and as a matter of fact, while I write—it is one o'clock in the morning—potatoes are cooking on the stove in front of me).

I have been told it is better for the water to be salted, strongly—not essential, but better.

A hubbub can be heard: the bubbling of the water. It is furious, or at least at a peak of excitement. It thrashes around angrily, steaming, oozing, sizzling, pfutt, tsitt; in short, terribly agitated on the red-hot grate.

My potatoes, submerged down there, are shaken up, knocked around, abused, drenched to the marrow.

The water's fury probably has nothing to do with them, but they suffer the consequences—unable to get out of this situation, they find themselves profoundly changed by it.

In the end, they are left for dead, or at least battered. If their form survives (which is not always the case), they have become soft and tender. All sourness has disappeared: their taste is good.

Their skin has also undergone rapid change: it has to be removed (it's good for nothing now) and thrown away . . .

There remains this tasty crumbly mass—lending itself to experiencing first, and philosophizing later.

1941

▣ Wine

The relationship between a glass of water and a glass of wine is the same as between an apron of cloth and an apron of leather.

And it may well be through tannin that wine and leather are related.

But there are other resemblances between them, equally deep: the stable and the tannery are never far from the cellar.

It is not exactly underground that one goes for wine, but still under ground level: the cellar is a kind of grotto.

Wine is the product of human patience, patience without much activity, applied to a sweetish murky pulp, dubious in color, and unstimulating.

Its inhumation and maceration in the darkness and humidity of cellars or grottoes, below ground level, produces a liquid that has all the opposite qualities: clear ruby through and through.

In this connection, I might say something about the kind of industry (or transformation) that consists of placing matter in the right place, in the right contact . . . and waiting.

An aging of tissues.

Wine and leather are about the same age.

Adults (already on the wane).

Both serve the same end: partial protection.

Both numb the extremities about the same way. Slowly. At the same time, they liberate the soul (?). It takes a certain amount.

Spirits and steel are of another temper; colorless besides. And less is needed.

The arm pours a cold puddle into the stomach, from which there immitaely arises something in the nature of a servant whose duty is to close all windows, darken the house, and light the lamp.

Lock up the master with his imagination.

The last-slammed door resounds endlessly, and from then on, the lover of red wine walks through the world as though through an echoing house, whose walls reply harmoniously to his steps,

whose railings twist like morning-glories under his exhaled breath, and everything applauds, rings with applause and reply to his bearing, his gesturing, his breathing.

The approval of everything twining around him weights his limbs. As ivy entwines a trellis, a drunk entwines a lamppost, and vice versa. Surely, the growth of climbing plants involves a similar drunkenness.

Wine is really not all that great. Yet its flame dances in many a body around town.

Dances more than it glows. Makes others dance more than it burns or consumes.

Transforms jointed bodies into puppets, mummers, marionettes.

Warms the limbs, livens the tongue.

Like all things, wine has a secret, but not long kept. One can make wine spill it: one need only love it, drink it, put it inside oneself. And it talks.

Talks in full confidence.

Whereas water keeps its secret; at least it's harder to unlock, take hold of.

1943–1946

◻ The Earth

(Let's just pick up a clod)

This moving mixture of the past of the three kingdoms, all of them spanned, infiltrated, trodden by their seeds and roots, their living avatars: that is earth.

This hash, this forcemeat containing the flesh of the three kingdoms.

Past, not as memory or idea, but as matter.

Matter within anyone's reach, even a baby's; that can be seized by the handful, the shovelful.

If speaking this way of the earth makes me a miner, or earthy, poet, that's just what I want to be! I don't know any greater subject.

While talking about History, someone grabbed a handful of earth and said: "Here's all we know about Universal History. But this we really know, we see, we hold, we have well in hand."
What veneration in these words!

Here too is our aliment; here is where our aliments are prepared. We settle on it as though on History's silos, each clod containing, in seed and root, the future.

For the present, here is our house and garden: the flesh for our houses, the ground for our feet.
And our material for modeling, our toy.
It will always be there for us. We only have to stoop to get some. And it doesn't soil.

It is said that within geosynclines, under enormous pressure, stone is formed anew. Well then, if one is formed, of a particular nature, that is, of earth in the proper sense of the word (improperly called vegetable matter), of those sacred remains, I'd like to see it! No diamond could be more precious!

Here then, is the present image of what we are likely to become.
And in this way are the past and the future present.
Everything has gone into it: not only the flesh of the three kingdoms, but the action of the other three elements: fire, air and water.
And space, and time.

What is completely spontaneous in man as he touches the earth is an immediate feeling of familiarity, sympathy, or even veneration, of a filial kind.

Because earth is matter to the highest.

So then, veneration of matter: is anything more fitting for the spirit?

Whereas spirit venerating spirit . . . can you see that?

—One sees only too much of it.

1944–1949

IV

from Lyres*

* LE GRAND RECUEIL, vol. I, Paris, Gallimard, 1961.

▣ Reflections on the Statuettes, Figures and Paintings of Alberto Giacometti

The moment has come, I think, to startle our generation by presenting it with a gripping truth—the most poignant one it can conceive of—which it had to formulate entirely by itself before we could do so. The smallest statuette by Giacometti is formal proof of this: for a generation—ours—to display its *stamens* so gloriously, it must have reached the end of its *flowering*.

Giacometti was born in 1901 in the mountain village of Stampa (Switzerland), which is to say in the rugged heart of Europe, but oriented more toward Italy. His mother, a rock (whom he resembles), married a field of flowers (a painter who, I have been told, was the finest Swiss exponent of the Impressionist school); she had three sons, like Switzerland herself: a rock and two pines.

It was thus in the most ordinary way that Alberto, born into an age of objets d'art, was determined to become an artist; he was sent to the Academy. But he was endowed with the only quality which enables one to produce a few masterworks: passionately sensitive to the world, or perhaps to certain things in the world, or perhaps to a certain thing in the world, he desired it with such fervor, such respect, such scruples, that he must have known the most pervasive torment because of it—and the absurdity of its expression. It is here that the profoundest questions arise. Why become a sculptor? He then decided to become himself.

Others in our generation were similarly slow to reveal themselves—in whatever way they could, in their own way. Not because they were less gifted, or less sensitive: one realizes that only now.

They simply confined themselves to the core, stem-like, long hidden by the brighter, faster falling offshoots. These latter (of whom I am less willing to speak), who by their convergent meeting formed at first the flowering point and for a while were the most splendiferous, are already withered. They now serve as kindling wood for the stewpots of bumpkins—whereas the others are still respected, ever since one has recognized the seedlings of life in their height. They will not be done away with easily. Later, they will become the masts of ships—and long after, in the nights of the future, it is from them that the swaying stars will hang.

Why become a sculptor? Shepherds, you tell us:

> Louis' crook, Mary's crook,
> Whose fateful staff keeps our flocks
> Away from the wolves,
> Placing you in the same province of the skies as
> Virgo's scales,
> Is that a fitting award for you?*

Like all mountain shepherds, Giacometti was subject to apparitions, and throughout the same night never stopped until he had transformed them into shepherds' crooks. Like Jupiter perhaps, to hold the lightning in his fist? . . .

The operation—all the harder in that it involves a mere nothing, a twist: nothing but turning a SPECTER into a SCEPTER—probably requires no more than enormous mental effort, and a pocket knife.

At daybreak shepherds find themselves changed into rocks . . . Which is doubtless why one often sees, in the neighborhood of the Café de Flore, this rock, this broad hairy gray figure, wandering around, still marked with the stigmata of his night's torment, still terrified by those scrawny menacing silhouettes of spindly trees

* Malherbe, *Récit d'un Berger au Ballet de Mme. la Princesse d'Espagne.*

around him, or those goats. Indeed, between the sculptor
and his statuettes the relationship is the same as between
a cyclops and a sylph, as between Polyphemus and
Galatea: jutting desire, plummeting glance—a colossal
difference of proportions.

To speak of Giacometti and his work it was necessary
to wait until only one thing remained to be said, while
simultaneously keeping it away and holding it close.
The work moreover deserves conciseness. Even if it
means rolling a few heavy rocks around it to set it apart,
out of possessiveness.

Why then was I tempted at first to talk about it sub-
jectively? Why, seeing how different I consider myself
(and perhaps one couldn't be more different), did I
think I couldn't get far enough away from it? Better yet,
why did I think that any man, at the sight of the least
important of these sculptures, would have to have the
same impression? Perhaps I do know . . . The reason
appeared as in a dream, and it is this . . . Oh, I thought
I had it, but it always stays out of reach! Can we bring
it in a little closer? Our reasons from here on will necessarily be a bit blurred . . .

Of course, they are just like those apparitions.

Some people see them as "lumps of space . . ."*
Others . . . No, my dear! Gastronome though I know
you to be and very clever about it, no! Even if they
have shriveled on the fire of burning passion—and
judging by certain photographs the image does present
itself most irritatingly—no! It would be highly un-
fitting to see these figurines as skewered kidneys.
Enough, I beg you! Or you will begin to irritate me!

If we are to misally let it be only over philosophy . . .

* J.-P. Sartre.

Fashion legitimizes it, what's more, and the age justifies it. What kind of apparitions are these? Religious ones, evidently (but what is the shepherd's religion?), pertaining to the preoccupations of our generation, its anguish, its faith. And what is it that anguishes us? What is it that crucifies us? Of whom can we say, like Pascal of Jesus, that *he* will remain on the cross so long as the world endures, that there is nothing else to think about?

Man . . . The Human Person . . . The Free Person . . . The I . . . Both hangman and victim . . . hunter and hunted . . .

Man—and man alone—reduced to a thread—in the dilapidation and misery of the world—looking for himself—starting from zero.

Exhausted, fleshless, skeletal, naked. Wandering aimlessly in the crowd.

Man anguished by man, terrorized by man. Affirming himself for the last time in a priestly pose of supreme elegance. The pathos of the total exhaustion of the individual reduced to a thread.

Man on his pyre of contradictions. Not even crucified any more. Broiled. You were right, my dear.

Man on his sidewalk as though on burning sheet metal, unable to unstick his big feet.

Since the days of Greek sculpture—what am I saying, since Laurens and Maillol—man has done a lot of melting on that pyre!

Probably because since Nietzsche and Baudelaire the destruction of values has accelerated.

They drip all around him, his values, his fats; to feed the pyre!

Not only does man have nothing; he is nothing; nothing but this I.

No longer a noun . . . Only a pronoun!

It is this I that you have managed to stand up on its pedestal, its monstrous foot, dear Alberto.

This scrawny, vague apparition that stands at the beginning of most of our sentences. This imperious phantom.

Thank you!

For thanks to you, we hold on to him: man—wallower in intelligence; this scepter, this thread; our ultimate god.

Even under the name of NOMAN, he can no longer put out our eyes.

We have only to watch out, and watch over his agony.

1951

◼ Braque-Drawings*

Here is the first collection of Georges Braque's drawings, and the only one, as yet, in which one can see brought together a few samples of the graphic work of that great painter, whose universally admired canvases presently hang in the major museums and finest galleries of the world.

It is only now—that his painting has netted him over the years such incomparable fame, that it flourishes and radiates on so many walls—that a few of his drawings have been collected and that Georges Braque has authorized their reproduction and publication.

This in itself should give us an idea of Braque's atti-

* Braque, *Dessins*, Paris, Braun, 1950; reprinted in LE GRAND RECUEIL, vol. I.

tude toward drawings, and of the place he allots them
in his work, if, at first glance, the very nature of these
plates did not emerge clearly and did not suffice to indicate it.

These are obviously the drawings of a painter, always
executed with an eye toward a future painting, or to one
in progress.

Still, even if the artist grants them no more than the
status of notes or drafts, it surely behooves us to consider them with the interest warranted by documents of
singular importance.

If it is true that in our day the taste of the majority
has descended to the lowest level, to the point of provoking irrepressible nausea and at times even destroying
the pleasure of living, there are some who, by way of
compensation, have raised themselves to the summit,
which involves taking humane pleasure—even more than
in the works themselves—in the rare and moving qualities they reveal in their maker, and in almost preferring
to the masterworks these album leaves, these working
pages on which are inscribed in all their vividness the
ups and downs of the struggle with the angel, in short,
those daily communiqués of the holy war . . .

Seen in that light, collections in which the paintings of
a famous master are reproduced in color could not pos-
sibly satisfy the more refined art lover. However pleased
he may be to own them, he will never leaf through them
without some manner of apprehension or uncertainty,
even a curious kind of remorse.

In the presence of a book like this one, such feelings
are necessarily mitigated, and can even disappear completely.

Take, for example, the drawings of Leonardo, or Rem-
brandt, or other masters of the past, and consider their

excellent likelihood of enduring within the totality of their expression. We are not at all sure any longer of the painting of these masters. But we can be eternally sure of their drawings.

Here then, just as they will remain unchanged in centuries to come, are the primary signs, the authentic traces of one of the greatest artists of our own time. I would like them to be considered with the interest and reverence they deserve.

We know how much we owe Braque, and why so many of our finest minds are devoted to him.

During the early years of this century, which began in a climate of triumphant daybreak, which promised to become the century of the power of man, it was Braque who (along with Picasso) contributed most powerfully to the dawning of a new art.

Electricity, automobiles, airplanes, appeared at that time. The smallest village seemed rebuilt, bedecked with fresh linen. In the other arts Stravinsky, Joyce, the first issues of the *Nouvelle Revue Française,* made their appearance. The kaleidoscope did not stop turning, and each new combination was more dazzling than the last. The war of 1914–18 itself did little to interrupt this process . . . *Parade,* the Ballets Russes . . . This continued until about 1925, when the Exposition of Decorative Arts in Paris consecrated the triumph and popularization of Cubism.

What happened was that the sharpest minds of the time, "those giants, those geniuses," took advantage of this dawning climate to rethink thoroughly the problem of painting and to carry out the most important revolution it had undergone since the Renaissance. In this way, they laid the ground for a rhetoric and a style that might have borne fruit over more than a century.

Suddenly, however, everything changed. Shall we say, euphemistically, that the results of the war may have been disillusioning? Whatever the case, everything clouded over, became infiltrated with germs, bacilla, everything turned baroque. As though the dazzling kaleidoscope we mentioned earlier had turned suddenly into a miscroscope focused on some kind of germ culture . . .

"What kind of world are we living in!," the Surrealist leader André Breton exclaimed ceaselessly with his incomparable tone of tragic nobility in rebellion. What kind of world? Everyone soon found out. The horror of it became apparent to everyone as of the war in Abyssinia, Guernica, then the exoduses and exterminations that followed.

The century of the power of man became that of his despair. Since then, everyone feels in his body and his soul that we are living in a more atrocious age than any other, an age of the most horrible savagery.

We know what kind of explanations one still offers us, that *one* who is never short of explanations, and who only sees in the fiercest rebuttals to his intelligence an occasion for becoming even more infatuated with it.

But there were some who, henceforth, would no longer accept any, and would denounce as ridiculous and criminal any argumentation, wherever it came from—unless from their own deep instinct, that naïve intuition which each day's evidence confirmed, and to which, it really must be said, Braque *alone* has always been faithful.

Never, it would seem, from the time the world is a world, never has the world in the mind of man—and precisely, I suppose, from the time he began seeing the world as no more than the field of his action, the time and place of his power—never has the world *functioned* so little or so badly in the mind of man.

It no longer functions at all except for a few artists. And if it does function, it is only because of them.

Here then is what some few men feel, and from that moment their life is traced out for them. There is only one thing for them to do, one function to fulfill. They have to open up a workshop and take the world in for repairs, the world in pieces, as it comes to them.

From then on, any other plan is wiped out: it is no more a question of transforming the world than explaining it, but merely putting it back into running order, piece by piece, in their workshop.

Do you think we have gotten away from Braque, from his workshop, his drawings? Not at all. We are just getting in, on the contrary; and perhaps only as of now.

When one enters Braque's workshop, believe me, it is a bit like coming to one of those small-town mechanics, with whom many a driver has had dealings and has generally been well satisfied.

A number of vehicles are already standing at the back, still immobile for the moment. The man goes thoughtfully from one to the other, according to urgency or the efficient use of his time.

Quite clearly, this has to do neither with virtuosity nor amusement. It is merely a matter of putting them back into running order with the means available, often very limited.

That is when an inventive mind reveals itself, inventive but nothing less than maniacal and with no taste for system. It is always a case by itself. And each time, of course, everything begins with a feeling. But immediately . . . "I love," says Braque as early as 1917,

"the rule that corrects the feeling." And what is this rule
if not the fitting together of the parts and their submis-
sion to the whole? Since, indeed, all that matters is the
whole, and that it function. But for that, must one sacrifice the parts? Evidently not, since the whole is made up
of parts, and it is always because of some part that the
rule is broken. Our man will therefore forge a piece as
needed, file some other one, twist a wire, invent a joint.
But never, under any pretext, will you hear him cry out
EUREKA! It will never occur to him to stop at one of
these discoveries, take out a patent, or exploit it as a
system. For there are other vehicles waiting, for which
this system would not work.

And so everything begins with a feeling, and yet the
rule intervenes. But what does he think of that rule?
Well, he loves it. That is still another feeling.

Here then is a man to whom everything comes spontaneously: the feeling, the rule that corrects it, and immediately thereafter, the love of that rule. Hardly surprising that he paints good pictures.

Sometimes, however, a slightly knottier problem
arises which requires more reflection. Reflection is
hardly the word. Let's see now; let's take some paper.
We then see our artisan leave his forge, his easel or his
pallette, and go over to his workbench where he clears a
space. He takes a pencil stub from behind his ear, takes
a scrap of paper, puts his problem on it, sketches his
drawing, finds his solution there.

Here one sees better than anywhere else, the closeness
of these two words: *dessein* (design) and *dessin* (drawing).

Dessein, dessin, design* . . . three forms of the same
word, once unified.

* Appears this way in the original.

What does Braque draw? His designs. At the same time precise yet imprecise. They are only designs. Just notes, but meticulous (though not polished). Proposals without self-satisfaction or boasting, merely tried out, thoughtfully, but if need be, withdrawn. A series of attempts, of errors calmly overcome, corrected. They have the manner and tone of study and research, never of conviction or discovery . . . But discovery is there, at every moment.

And then, back to the painting; the drawings remain on the workbench.

This, if you care to believe me, is how Braque's drawings should be understood, should be loved.

When all is said and done, this mechanic is merely a metaphor. It's not quite automobiles we're talking about.

In Braque's case, it is our whole world that is undergoing repair, is being reconditioned. It shudders and almost spontaneously starts up again. It resounds. The reconciliation has taken place. We are "in unison with nature." In time. In the perpetual "present." "The perpetual and its sound of origin."

"We will never be at rest." Probably not. But we are walking in step with time; cured.

◻ Drawings of Pablo Picasso
(Blue and Rose Periods)

*To Henri-Louis Mermod**

Dear friend,

You have said very much in few words and I congratulate myself on having convinced you to preface this album yourself, for, since the idea (and the desire to begin with) is yours, who better than you could present it to your readers. Why should I add to this? I saw little reason for this before, and even less now that I have read you.

Human likeness, delectation, dilection: these are your few words, well chosen perhaps even more for their coloring than for their literal meaning. My intention is manifestly clear: I shall merely set down a few returns of the ball you so adroitly threw me.

And what does that ball immediately remind me of? Even more than the ball of the *Acrobat with Ball* (1904), or the one manipulated (so to speak) by the feet of one of the members of the *Family of Acrobats* (1905), I am reminded of that lighter, multicolored beach ball left lying at the feet of the *Girl with Pigeon* (1901) which serves almost as an allegory of the painter's progress during that period.

Left lying for what, or rather for whom? For none other than the humble little ball of gray feathers rolled up in the hands of the wide-eyed child who clutches it tenderly to her heart.

---

* The Swiss publisher of the collection of drawings referred to (*Dessins de Pablo Picasso*, Lausanne, 1960) containing Ponge's prefatory letter, who published a number of Ponge's works. The letter was later reprinted in *Nouveau Recueil*, Paris, Gallimard, 1967.

Here is a true image of dilection.*

If we delve a bit deeper into the dictionary, as indeed
we should, we find that the root of dilection is *choice,* as
it also is of intelligence.

And what does Picasso choose at that time, this little
young man, though robust and agile, arriving in Paris
from Barcelona, eyes big and brilliant such as no one
in his generation has seen the likes of? He chooses
misery, in order to endear it. Because that is his likeness,
that is his fellow-creature.

It is, by the way, a taste that has never left him. *"You
like misery too much, Picasso!"* he was told more recently—already then a millionaire—by a sculptor-
friend from whom he had purchased a number of small
statues and who was offended to find them lying around
under furniture or in dusty drawers in the famous garret
of the Grands-Augustins. "I like misery!" the great
painter instantly retorted. *"If only it weren't so dear, I
could offer it to myself."*

But misery at the time in question was *given* to him.

Picasso at that time *has* nothing, except his prodigious
talents. There are properties of being (innate) and
properties of having. The latter are like burdens whose
absence, or unloading, raises and exalts the former,
permits them to flourish.

Picasso at that time *is* nothing but a prodigy. He *has*
nothing but his love of nature and his instinct for beauty,
his incomparable passion for work despite his precocious
virtuosity, his endless trials despite his infallibility.

We see him here before his Herculean labors, before

---

* Dilection, thought archaic in English, had to be retained for
evident reasons of wordplay (dilection—spiritual, reverent love, as
opposed to delectation—sensuous pleasure, delight). The Latin
roots referred to in the following paragraph are: *diligere,* to prefer; *intelligere,* to choose among.

he became the demigod, the hero, that Cubism and his
later works were to make of him.

Capable of everything, as are all great artists, he is
to begin with, as are only the greatest among the great,
capable of pity, tenderness, anguish, followed by defiance of anguish and soaring in the game, the great
game. Cursing and snickering, violence and vindictive-
ness only come later.

God (and great minds) are liable to indifference,
detachment, and consequently cruelty, knowing (too
well) how the world turns. But Picasso at that time is
not yet there. He is still only a man: as sensitive as an
animal, an angel, as adroit and clever as a monkey.

He lets himself go in his dilection and I might even
say his predilection for misery, and the blue or rose
tones it can assume.

I congratulated you earlier, my friend, on the coloring
of your well-chosen words. If human likeness resides
entirely, as I believe it does, in the miracle of an in-
fallible drawing, which most often encloses the most
neutral of tones, those of paper or cardboard, then the
contrast of those two exquisite words—dilection and
delectation—makes the second appear rose and the first
blue. I could prove it, if need be, but I think everyone
feels as I do.

Blue, in the vein of chance and mischance; rose, more
in the nature of flesh, or the faded leotard of the acrobat, that dandy* of voluntary penitence and the game of
chance.

And just as I was rejoicing over the profound ap-
propriateness of the word "dilection" whose root is
choice, I might point out, still on the level of the dictionary, that the root of "delectation," as of "delight,"

* In the Baudelairean sense.

is *delacire*—to ensnare, catch in a trap of laced string, which generally applies to drawings, and particularly to drawings of the type we are talking about: simple yet perplexing, like the windings of string.

However, it is time for me to return to the question of human likeness (which you rightly oppose to social or psychological likeness), for that is the essential thing, that is what the game is about.

Picasso's Blue and Rose works are not the ones, as I intimated above, which secure him the place in Parnassus that he will achieve shortly after, by his Herculean labors (Cubism), when he has chosen the heroic path indicated to him by Cézanne.

Nevertheless, he already possesses, right from the start, the qualities that ultimately enable him to choose that path.

Granted, he falls under the influence of the Parisian satirists as well as of the Symbolists. But his instinct for beauty, the superior balance of his genius, his spontaneity, his simple wholesomeness, make it possible for him to transcend these influences and surpass the best in both—Lautrec in the first, Gauguin in the second—and to express everything at once. If he expresses his anguish in solitude (Blue Period), then his defiance of anguish and his escape in the poetry of adventure (Rose Period), he does it without moving an inch outside of reality. No horrible toiler* in him, no muse. No groaning, no praying, no ecstasy.

Merely the simplest of gestures: leading a horse, hugging a bird, waiting in shirtsleeves arms behind back, raising a hand in greeting, lowering the other one that holds a closed fan, holding a child's hand with the right hand while the left holds the strap of a knapsack over

* Allusion to Rimbaud's *Lettre du Voyant*.

the shoulder, resting a hand on the head of a dog who rubs against your leg—and even more, the look in the eyes; everything is expressed, without a trace of pompousness; the eternal human condition; everything assumes the character of an inevitable ritual; the noble and shattering quality of destiny.

"In each figure and in a sublime aspect he unveils the inherent in it"—Apollinaire said of Ingres, whose name had to be mentioned here. Don't you agree? This applies equally to Picasso, and you were perfectly right to call it that: human likeness.

Affectionately yours,

V

The Prairie*

* *Nouveau Recueil*, Paris, Gallimard, 1967.

◱ Notes on The Making of the Prairie*

Ponge's poetic journal, *La Fabrique du Pré*, records not only the evolution of the poem's anatomy, but more important, the thought process of its creator, which is what fleshes out the poetic skeleton. Starting in August 1960 with the desire to write on the subject—"Ce que j'ai envie d'écrire c'est *Le pré*, un pré entre bois (et rochers) et ruisseau (et rochers)"—Ponge begins a series of reflections on the origin and nature of the prairie.

A metamorphosis of water and earth, that is, rock reduced to tiny fragments and mixed with all manner of debris from the other kingdoms, vegetable and animal. The whole reduced to infinitesimal grains—and *bedded down*. Which nonetheless stand up and flourish.

Grass is the upright flourishing progeny of these waterbound remains: "a million little breathing pumps that one can press but not repress," laying down its own pipelines, stretching out flat like a printer's plate, a color plate, a reposing color, a bed of color, "and not only the color, but the form invites one to stretch out on it." Crushable but not breakable, the resilient green surface is "a single layer of paint. The underside comes through. Thus it is even more precious than the finest of Persian rugs."

Each image engenders a new thought, a reminiscence: "A partir d'ici sur ma page, voici le galop. Le galop de l'écriture, selon l'inspiration." Moving from one art analogue to another (the color plate, Chagall's *pré*, Persian rugs), Ponge is reminded of Rimbaud's "clave-

---

* Since rights for partial translation of *La Fabrique du Pré* were not obtainable, I have provided the above notes as a compromise measure to grant the reader at least a glimpse of this "work in progress" which covers four years and 65 pages.—B. A.

cin des prés" ("Soir historique" in *Les Illuminations*).
The musical analogy seems to him very apt "because in
fact the prairie does sound like a harpsichord in contrast
to the organ sounds of the nearby forest or continuous
melody, the strings of the brook." The thin, short-sounding quality of the harpsichord suggests to him the short-
stemmed grasses and flowers of the prairie, a field as
varied as the tonal variations of the keyboard.

A refined, delicate pleasure, though almost prosaic: tedious,
less lyric than the organ or the strings (in one of the Bach
Brandenburg concertos a very long, varied, insistent, and
tedious-in-its-thinness passage of solo harpsichord); on a par
with the word, the human voice; rushed or slow, the same
rhythm; none of the soaring of the violin, none of the throbbing
of the organ; it would seem to come from the mind and the
lips, not the heart or the body (the guts) . . .

Another "galop," from the nature of the thing to the
word itself, leads him back to the fifteenth-century com-
poser, Josquin des Prés; the medieval Pré-aux-Clercs
and Saint-Germain-des Prés, the former emplacement of
the University of Paris, with its evocation of clerics,
scholars, disputations, duels, and today, district of
antique shops. Going even farther back, Ponge now
decides it is time to consult the dictionary. *Pré* is a tract
of land for hay or pasture; *Pré-aux-clercs*, a field for
scholarly disputation; *sur le pré*, dueling field and moment of decision: *rente de pré*, land revenue—all of
which come from the Latin *pratum* (pl. *prata*), whose
origin is obscure. "Nothing in all of this of any interest,"
says Ponge, "not definition, history, or etymology. But
Virgil says, "Sat prata biberunt."* That is meaningful.
Fields saturated with water . . . Is it the only word in
French from the same family [others listed are *prée*

---

* Ecologue III: "Now then boys, close the sluice gates, the fields
have drunk enough."

and *préau*]? Certainly not; there is also *prairie*, which is a terrain covered with herbaceous plants for grazing or cutting, hence synonymous with *pré*, which comes from the Vulgar Latin *prataria* for *pratum*."

Since the dictionary yields so little for *pré*, Ponge is inspired to try another tack. Perhaps there is some relationship to be found between the word and its homonyms, *près* (near) and *prêt* (ready).

Let us look first at *près*. The plural *prés* and the adverb *près* differ only in the direction of the accent (grave or acute), the direction of the bird flying over. *Près*, close in time or space, from the Latin *pressum* (*pressare:* to press, squeeze, push, crowd—doesn't that apply to the grasses of the prairie?). And now *prêt*, ready, prepared for, from the Latin *praestus*. *Praestare* means to furnish (in the sense of allocate). The noun *prêt* is a loan, of money or something else. No attempt is made to explain it. How curious! Nowhere is it related to *paratus*, readied, outfitted.

And yet, it is this origin which Ponge intuits as the reason behind the phonetic proximity of the three words with which "I shall define my *pré*."

Près (near) both rock and rill, brook, woods and river.
Prêt (ready) for grazing or mowing, ready also to serve as a
  place for rest or leisurely strolling.
Prêt (loan) from Nature to man and animals . . .
Compare also to *prairie*.
Pré is short: freshly cut or mown, never very tall, but upright.
  And its *é* has all the value of the diphthongs *ai* and *ie* in
  prairie.

From the etymological possibilities of *pré*, Ponge first extracts its physical qualities, then its associative qualities. It is a place of disputation, decision and brief combat, of death and rebirth. Its own brief dimensions (limited by rocks and hedges), its plants short of stalk relate to man's dimensions (short of life, short-sounding speech)—"Everything is a question of scale. The prairie is drawn to our scale." It evokes the billiard table (French slang, *le billard*, for operating table), the green baize of the conference table, the field of action for duelists and thinkers, and of repose for vagabonds and dreamers, nymphs and strollers. And finally the word itself, in its own brevity (even its homonyms: drop the *s* from *près* and the *t* from *prêt*), is "reduced to the value of a prefix, and even more precisely, the prefix of prefixes, the prefix par excellence, that sounds like a single plucked chord."

The associations are innumerable. Many are discarded, many are repeated, reworked, and eventually appear in the finished poem. But there are numerous fragments that never reappear, such as this one from 1963, except as a shadowed reference.

Ready to give up
stretched out on this prairie
and almost decided to move no more
To remain silent
To die here on top
So as to be placed below
without having to make another move
The sudden awareness
of the verticality of grass
the constant insurrection of green
resuscitates us . . .
Such is the *lyricism* of prairies,
the *organism* of prairies
(in the sense that *organism* is the same as *organ*) *

The entries of 1964 mirror the struggle to complete the poem in a back and forth movement that corresponds to the action of memory in conflict with the poet's verbal inspiration.

A rug of rest engendered by a brown page.
This rug of rest and platter of repast was not laid down.

* *orgue* in the French, the musical instrument, not *organe*.

Rather it is the progeny of a page of brown earth . . .
Suddenly little grains, sands of erudition germinated there.
This rug of rest, of discouragement and resurgence, will
it grow too fast? Let us shear it, mow it as close
as possible.
Let there only be the brown page and grass that in truth
is green.
Let there only be short grass on brown earth; let the
truth today be green.

The problem is to keep the poem as serenely pure as the
original experience. But the poetic imagination has a
way of galloping off into word plays (like *verité* [truth]
and *verte* [green]) and thought associations: "the sands
of erudition have germinated."

No way to get out of it
Even though this is the place where everything that
ends begins again . . .
No need to get out . . . of our original onomatopeias.
Their variety suffices to prove the complexity and
the truth of life and the world. But they have still
to be spoken. Said. And perhaps parabolized.
All of them to be told. To have been told.

He moves forward setting down lines that will stand,
then goes back to the early etymological impulse, and
even to the memory of the inception of the poem (or
essai as he calls it, in the double sense of attempt and
genre), noted for the first time in the journal on June
22, 1964!—a day after the lines quoted above were
entered. Walking through a pine grove with his wife,
"was it a Sunday?" in 1960, he perceived a prairie
stretching alongside a little river with groups of strollers
on it. "That was all. Nothing more . . . I was, I don't
know why, taken with a kind of enthusiasm, secret, calm,
pure, tranquil. I knew immediately that this vision
would remain as it was, intact in my memory. And that
I had to try and tell it. To understand it? Understand is

not the word. To try and hold on to its promised delight
and to penetrate it, communicate it. Why?"

The answer is clear in an entry that dates from the
final month of the journal, July 1964.

The prairie, then, is hope, resurrection, in its most elemental,
unique, ingenuous sense, but stretched horizontally before our
eyes for our relaxation, our repose. It is the field of our rest
prepared (*préparé*)—past participle comprising all elements,
all past action, and memory, the remembrance of the totality
of past actions. Totality, the field into which have entered the
remains of the three kingdoms. Accumulation of past days and
principle of today's day.

▣ The Prairie

When Nature, at our awaking, sometimes
	proposes to us
Precisely what we were intending,
Praise at once swells in our throats.
We think we are in paradise.

So it was with the prairie I wish to tell of,
And which provides my subject for today.

Since this has more to do with a way of being
Than with a platter set before our eyes,
The word is more fitting than paint
Which would not do at all.

Taking a tube of green and spreading it on the page
Does not make a prairie.
They are born in another way.

They surge up from the page.
And the page should furthermore be brown.

Let us then prepare the page on which today
    may be born
A verdant verity.

Sometimes then—we might also say in some places—.
Sometimes, our nature—
I mean by that Nature on our planet
And what we are each day on awaking—
Sometimes, our nature has prepared us (for) a
    prairie.

But what is it that blocks our way?
In this little underbrush half-shade half-sun,
Who sets these spokes in our wheels?
Why, as soon as we emerge over the page,
In this single paragraph, so many scruples?

Why then, seen from here, this limited fragment of
    space,
Stretched between four rocks or four hawthorn hedges,
Barely larger than a handkerchief,
Moraine of the forests, downpour of adverse signs,
This prairie, gentle surface, halo of springs
and of the original storm sweet sequel
In unanimous anonymous call or reply to the rain,
Why does it suddenly seem more precious to us
Than the finest of Persian rugs?

Fragile but not frangible,
The soil at times reconquers the surface,

Marked by the little hooves of the foal that galloped
    there,
Trampled by the cattle that pushed slowly toward the
    watering place . . .
While a long procession of Sunday strollers, without
Soiling their white shoes, moves ahead
Following the little stream, swollen by drowning or
    perdition,
Why then, from the start, does it prohibit us?

Could we then already have reached the naos,
That sacred place for a repast of reasons?
Here we are, in any case, at the heart of pleonasms
And at the only logical level that befits us.
Here the prayer wheel is already turning,
Yet without the slightest idea of prostration,
For that would be contrary to the verticalities of the
    place.

Crasis of *paratus,* according to Latin etymologists,
Close [*près*] to rock and rill,
Ready [*prêt*] to be mown or grazed,
Prepared for us by nature,
Pré, paré, près, prêt.

The prairie [*pré*] lying there like the ideal past
    participle
Is equally rever(d)end as our prefix of prefixes,
Pre-fix within prefix, pre-sent within present.

No way out of our original onomatopeias.
In that case, back into them.

No need, furthermore, to get out,
Their variations being adequate to account

For the marvelously tedious
Monotony and Variety of the world.
For its perpetuity, in short.

Yet must they be pronounced.
Spoken. And perhaps parabolized.
All of them, told.

. . . .

(Here a long passage should intervene—somewhat
like the interminable harpsichord solo of the 5th
Brandenburg Concerto, that is, tedious and mechanical,
yet at the same time mechanizing, not so much because
of the music as the logic, reasoning from the lips, not
the chest or the heart—in which I shall try to explain,
and I mean explain, two or three things: to begin with, if
pré, in French, represents one of the most important and
primordial of logical notions, it holds equally true for
the physical (geophysical), since what is involved is a
metamorphosis of water which, instead of evaporating,
at the summons of heat, directly into clouds, chooses
here—by clinging to the earth and passing through it,
that is, through the kneaded remains of the past of the
three kingdoms and particularly through the finest
granulations of the mineral kingdom, ultimately re-
impregnating the universal ashtray—to renew life in its
most elementary form, grass: element-aliment. This
chapter, which is *also* to be the music of the prairies,
will sound thin and elaborate, with numerous appog-
giaturas, so as to end (if it ends) both accelerando and
rinforzando, in a kind of thunderclap which makes us
seek refuge in the woods. The perfecting of this passage
could easily take me a few more years. However it turns
out . . .)

. . . .

The original storm spoke at length.

. . . .

Did the original storm not thunder so long within us
precisely so that
　　　　　　　　　—for it rolls away, only
　　　　　　　　　partially filling the lower
　　　　　　　　　horizon where it lightens still—
Readying for the most urgent, rushing to the most
　　　　pressing,
We would leave these woods,
Would pass between these trees and our remaining
　　　　scruples,
And, leaving behind all portals and colonnades,
Transported suddenly by a quiet enthusiasm
For a verity that might today be verdant,
Would soon find ourselves stretched out on this
　　　　prairie,
Long ago prepared for us by nature
　　　　　　　　　—where nothing matters any
　　　　　　　　　more but the blue sky.
The bird flying over it in the opposite direction to
　　　　writing
Reminds us of the concrete; and its contradiction,
Marking the differential note of *pré*,
Whether *près* or *prêt*, or the *prai* of prairie,
Sounds short and sharp like the tearing
Of meaning in the all too clear sky.
For the place of long discussion can just as well
Become the place of decision.

Of two equals standing on arrival, one at least,
After a crossed assault with oblique weapons,

Will remain lying,
First above, then below.

Here then, on this prairie, is the occasion, as befits,
To come to an end, prematurely.

Gentlemen typesetters,
Place here, I beg you, the final dot.

Then, beneath, with no spacing added, lay my name,
In lower case, naturally,
     Except the initials, of course,
     Since they are also the initials
     Of Fennel and Parsnip which
     Tomorrow will be growing up on top.
    Francis Ponge

VI

This Is Why
I Have Lived*

* This previously unpublished poem (except in manuscript facsimile) appears here through the kindness of the author, who graciously approved my edition and translation of his manuscript.

◻ This is Why I Have Lived
Les Fleurys
night of 19-20 July, 1961

Taking an intense pleasure in doing nothing
but provoking (by my mere presence
charged with a kind of magnetism
for the being of things; this presence being
in some way exemplary: through the intensity
of its tranquillity (smiling, indulgent),
through the power of its patience,
the power of the example of its existence
accomplished in tranquillity, in repose,
through the power of the example of its health)
but provoking an intensification
of the true, authentic, unadorned nature
of beings and things;
nothing but awaiting it, awaiting that very moment

Doing nothing but awaiting
their particular declaration
And then fixing it, immobilizing it, petrifying it
   (Sartre calls it) for eternity, fulfilling it or
better yet helping it (without me it would not be
   possible) to fulfill itself.

Doing nothing but writing slowly black on white
—very slowly, attentively, very black on very white.

I stretched out
alongside beings and things
Pen in hand, my writing table
(a blank page) on my knees.

I have written, it has been published, I have lived.
I have written, they have lived, I have lived.

Bibliography

1962   *Douze Petits Ecrits*
1942   *Le Parti Pris des Choses*
1948   *Prôemes; Le Peintre à L'Etude*
1952   *La Rage de L'Expression*
1950   *La Seine*
1961   LE GRAND RECUEIL
       I. *Lyres*
      II. *Méthodes*
     III. *Pièces*
1965   *Pour un Malherbe*
1967   *Le Savon; Nouveau Recueil*
1970   *Entretiens de Francis Ponge avec Philippe
       Sollers* (Edited Transcripts of Twelve
       Radio Interviews).
1971   *La Fabrique du Pré*

▣ Selected Critical Works

IN FRENCH

JEAN-PAUL SARTRE, "L'Homme et les choses," *Situations* I, Gallimard, Paris, 1947.

Nouvelle Revue Française, Paris, September 1956. The
entire issue was devoted to articles on Ponge and in-
cludes Albert Camus' "Lettre au sujet du Parti pris
des choses."

JEAN THIBAUDEAU, *Ponge*, La Bibliothèque Idéale, Gallimard, Paris, 1967. The most complete biography-
analysis to date.

IN ENGLISH

BLOSSOM DOUTHAT, "Francis Ponge's Untenable Goat,"
Yale French Studies, no. 21, 1958.

BETTY MILLER, "Francis Ponge and the Creative
Method," *Horizon*, XVI, 1947.

N. M. WILLARD, "A Poetry of Things: Williams, Rilke,
Ponge," Comparative Literature, XVII, 1965.

DAVID PLANK, "Le Grand Recueil: Francis Ponge's
Optimistic Materialism," *Modern Language Quarterly*, 26, 1965.

MARK TEMMER, "Francis Ponge: A Dissenting View of
His Poetry," *Modern Language Quarterly*, 29, 1968.

TRANSLATIONS (in book form)

Soap, translated by Lane Dunlop, Grossman, New York,
1969.

Things, selected pieces translated by Cid Corman, Grossman, New York, 1971.